When Eagles Soared

by HARRY COOPER

First Printing September 2010
Copyright 2010 by Harry Cooper
All rights reserved by the copyright holder

Pertinent portions of this book may be used in reviews or quoted in scholarly papers without violation of copyright laws if the author's name, book title and contact web address are listed as the source.

Sharkhunters International
P. O. Box 1539 Hernando, FL 34442

www.sharkhunters.com

Harry Cooper*When Eagles Soared*

YOU can be published in our Sharkhunters Books

We welcome any factual stories and any wartime photographs you wish to send to us. Feel free to send to us at the address on the previous page and you will see your name in print in a subsequent Sharkhunters book.

NOTE – Portions of this book were written by others, named in the table of contents. Author Harry Cooper combined these portions.

DEDICATION & THANKS

This book is dedicated to all who lost their lives in aerial combat in the skies during World War II. It seems impossible that another war of the magnitude of WW II could ever happen again and it is virtually impossible that the deeds of the individual combatants could ever again be experienced. Warfare is now more of a computer game than the man against man, ship against ship or plane against plane combat that was the norm for World War II.

While no sane person wants or enjoys war, we must remember those who did their part for their country and who fought honorably for their homeland. There was a spirit of camaraderie, friendship and fun at times while there was despair and terror at other times. It is only by the people who were there and who tell their stories that the real history and the actual '*flavor*' of the era can be saved for all time.

To our Sharkhunters Members who took the time and effort to send their memories by audiotape, videotape, typed or hand-written, we extend our heartfelt thanks. Their memories of the War at Sea will be permanently preserved in history for all time not as the deductions and assumptions of hobbyists or aficionados who never tasted battle – but rather as the first person memories of those who did; the warriors of World War II.

About Sharkhunters

Sharkhunters is the largest research center and publication in the world covering the history of the German U-Bootwaffe of the 2nd World War and is a leader in Luftwaffe history. In our monthly **KTB** Magazine, we cover a great deal of aviation history of WW II with emphasis on the Luftwaffe.

Our website www.sharkhunters.com will give you additional information.

INTRODUCTION

Germany was destroyed, devastated, broken and helpless under the victorious Allied powers after World War One. The ill-conceived Treaty of Versailles had a boot on the German throat. They were allowed a small defensive military not to exceed 100,000 troops and no more than 800 officers. An Air Force was not in the big picture yet.

Carefully the Luftwaffe was rebuilt, bringing the best and brightest fliers into the force. They gave far better than they got during the Spanish Civil War which, in the minds of many researchers, was a testing ground for German pilots and planes. It was highly successful and when World War Two broke out, there were a great many pilots with skills honed sharp by great combat experience. Join us now as they tell us of their memories.

They had the hottest planes, the best pilots and they ruled the skies – for a time. Then technology in other countries moved rapidly forward while the German technology did not keep up. Couple that with the Allied attacks on the fuel industry and manufacturing factories, and the Luftwaffe was bled to where it was unable to put planes into the air in sufficient numbers to combat the enormous bomber streams in the skies.

Return with us now to a time when men took to the skies in the hunt for their enemy fighter pilots – and only one of the two would return.

HARTMANN

RALL

ROELL

Introduction to the Author

I was a kid during the war years and I loved to follow the air combat on the nightly radio broadcasts. I knew every kind of fighter, bomber, recon plane in the skies for any nation and I just knew I wanted to be a fighter pilot more than anything. I was just turning six when World War Two ended so I wasn't going to get into that one; same for Korea. I joined the U.S. Air Force right out of high school, stupidly assuming that I would go right into flight school. I guess recruiters are not totally honest……..

So, after basic training at Lackland AFB, I shipped to Lowrey AFB outside Denver and spent six months in intensive training on weapons. My specialty was thermonuclear weapons so I spent almost three years in charge of a crew of six men loading hydrogen bombs onto B-47 bombers.

Finally I was close to my 21st birthday so I took the Officer Candidate School examination and was the only one out of thirty to pass the tough two-day-long battery of tests, and I had near perfect scores. I was going to be a fighter pilot! On my own I went to the base hospital for a pilot's physical. Perfect! For sure I was going to be a fighter pilot now!

Not so fast! The career counselor gave me the sad news that the Air Force had so many pilots left over from WW II and Korea they had shut down Air Cadets! I could be an officer, not a pilot. I took my discharge instead.

Then I remembered something I had read in an Air Force magazine at a fantasy flightline and imaginary pilots. First a Spad flew over and landed. In a few minutes, a rugged P-40 Warhawk landed and taxied to where the men were standing. Then a sleek P-51 Mustang landed and the pilot joined the others. Next was an F-86 Saberjet and the pilot, a little older than the others, joined the men. A screaming F-100 Super Saber was next to land and that pilot, even a little older, joined the other pilots.

They waited and watched, but no others came. The last line in the article was, *"The fighter pilots were gone. There were no more fighter pilots."*

I realized that this was true – there really were no more fighter pilots. Gone were the brave young WW I guys with leather helmets and jackets with white silk scarf flowing behind them. Gone were the kids in their late teens that lived hard on the edge in WW II and died in their fast, powerful propeller driven fighters. Gone too were the first fighter pilots of the jet age. What was left? Where were the fighter pilots?

There were no more fighter pilots. There were no more men who saw their adversary through a spinning propeller, no more of the early jet jockeys who saw their opponent through their windscreen.

They had been replaced by high flying, high speed computer operators who rarely saw their target – they saw a display on a radar set and when it gave them the indication to fire – they pressed a button then headed back to base for coffee, knowing that they had sent a missile off to hit an unseen plane flown by a pilot who didn't see them either.

The 'man versus man' aspect was gone and I realized that I'd have been a miserable fighter pilot if I'd stayed around long enough for flight school. I had to accept the fact that I was born about 20 years too late.

After college and beginning to make my way up the corporate ladder, I found something almost as good as being a fighter pilot. It had all of the man versus man thrills of aerial combat, the high speeds – I became a professional racing driver…..they didn't let us mount guns on the cars.

But it sure was fun!

A Very Special THANKS!

The author believes that this "**Thank You**" should be in a separate section all its own. We wish to extend our most sincere and heartfelt thanks to all the veterans of all sides who gave their stories to Sharkhunters and only to Sharkhunters. They knew we worked very hard to tell the true and honest history of the Luftwaffe and of the men who lived and died in the skies.

They were not the raving maniacs who machine gunned men in their chutes for sport; they did not hate God and pray to Adolf Hitler and they were not radical Nazis. They were decent, patriotic young men really in love with their country, their planes and with air combat itself. These were the Knights of the Skies; they lived and died with great honor.

Return with us now to those glory days in the skies during World War Two when daring young men in their powerful planes lived the life so many dreamed of; young men with whom the young ladies fell in love; young men who did not always finish their tour of duty.

To these brave pilots, no matter in what uniform, we say 'Thanks!'

TABLE OF CONTENTS

CHAPTER		PAGE
1	*"Foo Fighters"* I	10
2	**Flying Combat with the Luftwaffe I**	16
3	**Not Good to Sink your own Submarine**	30
4	**the 'Black Devil'**	35
5	**A Mystery Solved**	40
6	**First Trans-Atlantic Flight**	45
7	**A Secret Kept**	49
8	*"Foo Fighters"* II	55
9	**by a Pubic Hair**	58
10	**Luftwaffe Memories I** German Secret Weapons – FRITZ-X	61
11	**Surviving Under Duress** Was Graf a Coward?	66
12	**the Gallant Galland**	70
13	**Flying Combat with the Luftwaffe II**	74
14	**the Disastrous Kassel Mission**	79
15	**the WALRUS** (What the hell is THAT?)	96

TABLE OF CONTENTS (continued)
Post war interrogation of Großadmiral Karl Dönitz.

16	Flying Pigs in India	116
17	*AICHI M6A Seiran*	118
18	Both Sides of the Same Coin (the Colin Kelly Story)	121
19	Attack on Convoy PQ.18 (One of the worst convoy losses in WW II)	127
20	Flying Combat with the Luftwaffe III	144
21	The P-40 Fighter	150
22	The Luftwaffe's '*Throw Away*' Fighter	156
23	The Heinkel HE 177	164
24	My Three Great Escapes from the Communists	167
25	Flying Combat with the Luftwaffe IV	191
26	Ivan Kozhedub, Top Soviet ACE	196

A Special Thanks

To my wife Kay and to my kids, Sean and Meaghan. Their support while this book was underway was priceless.

CHAPTER 1

'FOO FIGHTERS I'

Was there a German 'Flying Saucer?"

By Sharkhunters Member Lou Mari

Lou was a decorated Green Beret Major in Vietnam

What were/are **'FOO FIGHTERS'**? In the late stages of World War II, pilots of both sides reported seeing strange flying objects which became known, at least to American pilots, as **'FOO FIGHTERS'**. Pilots of both sides thought these strange flying objects were a secret weapon of the other side and perhaps they were but who knows?

Here are Lou's thoughts on which he comments;

"Following is a brief synopsis of the *'FOO FIGHTER'* phenomenon which I believe was caused by both a natural occurrence called *BALL LIGHTNING* and the man-made phenomenon called **PLASMOIDALS**. At present, I tend to believe that the Germans had a go at creating flying **PLASMOIDALS** using the technology of the Serbian-American scientist Nikola Tesla with who they had a relationship since World War One"

IS THERE A GERMAN 'FLYING SAUCER'? MORE UNSOLVED QUESTIONS.

In the early postwar years the press, whether tabloids or quality papers, printed several similar-sounding articles on a secret German weapon, a so-called *'FLYING DISC'* which, by the end of WW II, was said to have reached the prototype state after a series of tests. In the article 'Is there a German *FLYING DISC'*, published in 1975, the author tried to dismiss this tale as science fiction. But obviously, this topic still persists. Only recently, a former pupil of pilot training school C 14 announced that he had actually seen one of these mysterious flying objects when participating in a course at Prag-Gbell (former called Prag-Kbely) in 1943.

In contrast to the previously vague reports by the yellow press, the aforesaid pilot is able to name various trainee pilots of his course along with their instructors who perhaps might have also viewed the event as our witness was not the only one to see the machine. Here is his report:

Place of observation - Pilot training school C 14 at the airfield Prag-Gbell.

Time of observation - August or September, 1943, probably on a Sunday (as I recall that there has not been any flying).

The weather - warm, sunny, dry

The observation - Together with several colleagues I was on the airfield standing next to the building where our course took place.

Distance to the maintenance area - approximately 200 meters. In the hangar a flying object, a disc with a diameter of 5 to 6 meters, was standing on its four high legs.

Its height - tall as a man.

Thickness of the disc: approximately 30 to 40 cm. Its rim was fan-shaped, perhaps they were square openings. The upper part of the fuselage (approximately one third of its total height) flared in flush with the disc, the bottom section was bulgy.

Could it be the forerunner of this experimental craft?

Together with my friends, I eye witnessed the machine being pushed onto the apron in front of the hall. Then we heard a loud crackling (a sound comparable to an old motorbike starting) and observed how the outer rim of the disc started to turn. The machine moved to the SE end of the airfield and took off, flying at a height of 1 meter. After 300 meters it touched down again. The landing was pretty rough. While several ground crew members pushed the machine back into the hangar, we were told to leave the airfield. Later, it was reported that the *'thing'* had flown again, then reaching the other end of the airfield.

According to entries in my logbook, signed by someone called Böhme, the personnel of FFS C 14 at that time consisted of group flying instructor Oberfeldwebel Michelsen, supported by the flying instructors Unteroffizier Kohl and Unteroffizier Buhler.

Trainee pilots were:
- Obergefreiter Klassmann,
- Obergefreiter Klavier,
- Obergefreiter Mullers,
- Obergefreiter Pfaffle,
- Obergefreiter Schenk,
- Obergefreiter Seifert,
- Obergefreiter Seibert,
- Obergefreiter Squaar,
- Obergefreiter Stahn,
- Obergefreiter Weinberger,
- Obergefreiter Zoberle,
- Gefreiter Hering,
- Gefreiter Koza,
- Gefreiter Sitzwohl,
- Gefreiter Voss and
- Gefreiter Waluda.

So far the observer's report. On the ground plan of Prag-Gbell airfield, featuring only the main buildings, the *'saucers'* flight path and the observer's location are marked. The rough drawing of the mysterious flying object is based both on its description and the alterations proposed. The machine described by our witness is much smaller than the gigantic 'flying saucer' attributed to Hebermohl, Miethe and Bellonzo - they name diameters of 14.4, 16, 42, 52 and even 75 meters. According to the characterization of the engine sounds, it must have been fitted with a much smaller power plant. Certainly, readers may now ask why this event has only been revealed 45 years later by the former pilot - but he might have had quite plausible reasons for his proceedings.

BALL LIGHTNING EXTERNAL TO AIRCRAFT

X1. General observations 'There are three kinds of these lights we call *'FOO FIGHTERS'* according to Lt. Donald Meiers.:
1. A red ball which appears off our wing tips and flies along with us.
2. A vertical row of three balls of fire, flying in front of us.
3. A group of about fifteen lights which appear in the distance, like a Christmas tree up in the air, and flicker on and off.

X2. May 15, 1970 - An aircraft 150 miles east of St. Louis, Missouri, in a thunderstorm at (what seemed) the moment of maximum turbulence and electrical discharge, while the aircraft was still descending through the storm, a sequence of events took place as listed below, though not necessarily in chronological order:
1. The turbulence ceased altogether;
2. The surrounding electrical discharges (glows) totally ceased;
3. The wings stopped buckling altogether;
4. A white glowing sphere (ball lightning??) appeared on the port wing tip. I do not know if it was actually touching the wing. Its diameter was less than 1 meter and more than 10cm. Its boundary was *'fuzzy'* and not distinct.
5. There was a soft *'pop'*.
6. The ball lightning (??) vanished.

X3. No date or place is given. A further important observation was of a 20cm ball which appeared at a height of about 50cm over the training edge of the mainplane of an aircraft in flight. It moved parallel to the line of the mainplane before being cast off the end and was not blown off, in spite of considerate air speed.

X4. April 23, 1964. An aircraft over Bedford, England. A loud bang and a whitish-blue flash of light. A ball of blue light the size of a football appeared on the starboard wing tip. It vanished in two seconds.

X5. No date or place given. In the second case, a bright ball appeared on the top surface of the wing outside the aircraft, made rapid movements to and fro for an appreciable length of time and then disappeared. It seemed quite unaffected by the air passing through it at 250 mph, which does not accord very well with the theory that the balls may be composed of vaporized metal.

X6. No date or place given. Describing the types of St. Elmo's Fire - the 'small ball' formation varies in sizes from two inches to a foot and a half in diameter, and generally *'rolls around'* the aircraft apparently unaffected by the movement of the aircraft. On one occasion a small ball (about 6 inches in diameter) of yellowish white lightning formed on the left tiptank in an F-94B then rolled casually across the wing, up over the canopy, across the right wing to the tiptank and then commenced a return, which was not noted by the pilot but was by the observer who also noted that it disappeared as spontaneously as it had appeared.

Sometimes the balls are blue, blue-green, or white though it appears to favor the blue-green and yellow-white.

X7. General observations - mysterious balls of fire follow Allied planes closely. No explosive or incendiary effects are noted.

X8. General observations - the same sort of fireballs followed aircraft in both the European and Pacific Theaters. B-29 pilots said they stayed about 500 yards off, were about 3 feet in diameter, had a phosphorescent glow, and could not usually be shaken off by maneuvering or flying into clouds. This report states that radar did not detect the *'FOO FIGHTERS'*.

CHAPTER 2

Flying Combat with the Luftwaffe I

Remembered by Sharkhunters Member and former Luftwaffe flier Baron Georg von Zirk. Here is his wartime CV:

Navigator/Bombardier; Pathfinder and Target Marker; 81 Combat Missions (65 were Night Ops); Service from 8 August, 1941 through 5 May, 1945. Prisoner of the Communists June 1945 through May 1947. Served with the *Afrika Korps* in Italy and in combat with *Kampfgeschwader 'GREIF'* and *KG 4 'General Wever'* (Bomber Wings) *IV Fliegerkorps, Luftflotte 6 IV Flying Corps, 6th Air Fleet*, Eastern Front.

My Close Calls and Survival in WW II.

It was the end of summer vacations. I was getting ready to go back to school. I had to change schools, because I had graduated and had to look for a school teaching professional skills. So on August 27th, I went by train to Warsaw, to look for a Technical College. When I checked at the school, I found out I was too late - all places were already filled. I made the best of it and visited family from mother's side. They were glad to meet me and showed me around the city. The weather was beautiful and people were enjoying themselves everywhere, not knowing that a few days later, disaster would strike and change their lives forever. I didn't know either and returned home two days before German bombs fell on Warsaw.

At that time, I and my family were living in Poland. They lived there since 1812 when my Prussian ancestor had to go with the French Army when Napoleon wanted to conquer Russia. He never made it back to his homeland in Brandenburg.

On September 1st, 1939 World War II began at 4:30 in the morning. I woke up from the roar of many airplanes. When I ran outside, it was heavy fog and I couldn't see anything. My parents were already there. We speculated that this must be war. Later, Radio Warsaw confirmed this. German bombers were attacking Warsaw. Soon the fog lifted and we could see the low-flying bombers returning.......several hundreds, in groups of 40 to 60 - it was an awesome sight.

Soon wagons of refugees were arriving at our farm, fleeing from the German Army. We gave them shelter and many slept on our kitchen floor.

One day, a low-flying bomber was attacking retreating Polish soldiers on the nearby highway. We could hear the machine guns. Another, returning from a mission, dropped his bombs in the nearby forest. We could see trees, blasted into the air like matchsticks. Next a squadron of Stukas arrived overhead.

They were circling for some time and fired machine guns into the sky. Suddenly, two went into a dive, straight towards our farm. I heard their sirens screaming (this sound became the terror of the War). It was very frightening and I took cover in some bushes. Luckily, no bombs were dropped this time. I will never forget the piercing whine of the sirens - the trademark of the Stuka.

In the evening of September 3, I heard loud clanking noises from the nearby highway. I went to investigate and saw a column of Polish tanks driving to the front to meet the Germans. On the 5th of September we could hear cannon fire. The Germans were closing in. It was my mother's birthday and she was crying. She feared it would be her last. We all didn't know what to expect and what would happen to us.

In the morning I saw the last Polish horse soldiers, galloping through our village. Later I saw a Polish reconnaissance plane high overhead. Suddenly, it turned around and left at full speed. At about 3 in the afternoon, I saw the German soldiers approaching on the nearby highway. I mounted my bike and rode to the highway. I wanted to see what was happening. I saw the spearhead, consisting of horsemen with their steel helmets and long sabers. They appeared to me like medieval warriors.

Several armored cars, personnel carriers with heavy guns followed, and then companies of infantry. They were all looking at me and were probably wondering; *what is this fool kid doing alone in a battle zone?* But nobody stopped me, and I rode the 3 kilometers into our town. There I saw many cars and soldiers passing through.

A large staff car drove up and stopped where I stood. In it I recognized a General by his uniform with red lapels and golden epaulets. It was probably General von Brock or von Runstedt (photo right), who led the campaign in Poland. They were making history and became famous during the course of the War.

I walked up to a young MP who was directing traffic at the crossroads. One was leading to Lodz, the other to Warsaw. When I spoke to him in German, he looked surprised. He didn't expect to meet a German lad in enemy territory. As we were talking, we heard a loud commotion.

Several cars were returning and raced into the marketplace. I heard a pistol shot and saw a civilian fall to the ground. A German officer, standing in his car, had shot him. Then the car was passing me and the pistol was aimed at me. I was standing there and just waiting for the next shot to ring out. The MP, seeing what was happening, jumped in front of me and covered my body with his body. This saved my life.

The cars raced on and returned. Again the gun was aimed at me and again the soldier covered me. This time, the officer had the car stopped and came after me on foot. Only after the MP had explained to him that I was German, he finally lowered his gun. It turned out that he was the Commander of the armored car unit which I had met on the highway before. They had driven into a Polish ambush and lost one car. This enraged this officer so much that he returned to town, bent on revenge. So I almost lost my life the very first day, when I met up with the Germans from the Reich.

The Polish campaign was over in 27 days.

The Germans began organizing the local German men right away, mostly for the SS and SA. But we could choose, and I went to the Flieger Korps (Flying Corps). I was sent for 3 months to pilot training on gliders and sail planes. I made my ABC ratings. Afterwards I attended 4 weeks of infantry combat training, where I earned the Wehrsportabzeichen in Bronze. As I was still attending school, they had to give me leave. At that time, paramilitary training was more important than learning.

We also had to take the Volksliste (declare our allegiance to the German Government). We got new ID's which made German citizens. Who ever refused ended up in a concentration camp. Every day we read long lists of men and women who had been shot for some trespasses like sabotage, subversive remarks against the Government, black marketeering, etc. Most of them were Poles, but it didn't matter. Everybody who was against the Nazi Government could expect no mercy. Such was the situation when I had to make my choice.

Actually, the Poles had done this for us already, when they were killing us in the weeks before the Germans arrived. They hated Hitler and Germans, and took it our on us Volksdeutsche (ethnic Germans). The bloodbaths in Lodz, Bromberg, Posen, Thorn and everywhere German communities existed are not mentioned in post-war history books. But we Germans in Poland - men, women and children lived and died through it by the ten thousands. 49,000 were brutally murdered. I lost four of my immediate family. They had been tortured and mutilated. We learned of the tragedy only after the Germans had arrived.

EDITOR NOTE – Georg is absolutely correct. History does not record the reason that Hitler sent troops into Poland on 1 September 1939. Tens of thousands of ethnic Germans were massacred by Polish authorities and civilians in August 1939 in the towns he mentions. Many such photos exist.

The War went on, with all the victory news of the *BLITZKRIEG* on radio every day I feared that I would '*miss the War*'. So I volunteered for the Luftwaffe and on 8 August, 1941 went to war. With this, my life would change forever. Sooner or later, everything would be lost. So much tragedy was to follow - 13 family members lost during the course of the War. The family farm of five generations lost, the homeland. But at that time, I didn't know. I thought that glory was waiting for me and I had to be there.

After my basic training in France, I wanted to become a fighter pilot. I passed all required tests and was accepted. My school buddy, Paul, and I were the only ones from the whole regiment. But there was a SNAFU and my papers were lost, and instead of going to pilot school I ended up at a ground unit at Stettin Airfield. Paul went on and became a fighter pilot, flying Me 109's. He was training for years (fuel shortage) and only in January 1945 came into combat. He died in the last days of the War.

A few weeks later, our Company was sent to Italy and assigned to the Afrika Korps. We were waiting for shipment to Afrika in Spring 1942, where Rommel had the British on the run from Tobruk to El Alamein.

I put in another request for transfer to Flight School and few weeks later was transferred to Flight PreSchool in Austria. There was more waiting. Because of fuel shortages as early as 1942, training at pilot schools was delayed for months at a time.....and we were supposed to win the War??? To keep us busy, we had more ground training. No, this was not the war I had dreamed of. Two months later, out unit was sent to the English Channel, just in time to take part in stopping the first Allied landing at Dieppe in 1942. We were attacked by a British Spitfire. The pilot made a low level pass on our Vierlingsflak (four barrel 2.0 cm automatic gun). A hit in the cockpit killed him instantly. His plane hit the ground and disintegrated as it skidded about 150 meters.

Lack of food. Supply Officers stealing?

In a few days everything was back to normal for us. This was more ground training and running obstacle courses. Our drill instructors were treating us badly. Many times we were gritting our teeth in frustration. There was always something new. For the first time we were going hungry in France where we could still buy watches and perfumes. Probably our Supply Officers were sending our rations home to their families?? We could barely survive on our food rations. Often we were volunteering for kitchen duty so we could eat the leftovers of the NCO's who were getting extra food stamps and didn't care for potatoes with spinach.

After months of this misery, suddenly came a break. From Flight School came a request for volunteers as trainees as Navigator-Bombardiers. I was with them when they left two weeks later. Training as Navigator-Bombardiers was very demanding and some guys could not keep up.

They were relieved and sent to gunnery school or *Falschirmjäger* (Paratroops).

We almost lost Georg!

One day, on a bomb training flight, I had a bad incident. After finishing my bomb run, I went to the rear and lay down in the gunnery station, which had an exit hatch. When the airplane dropped in an air pocket, the hatch suddenly opened accidentally and I slid halfway out. I just could grab hold on one side of the fuselage. My comrades pulled me back in. We were flying at 15,000 feet - and I had no parachute on.

In nine months, I finished my intensive training and was assigned to a combat group, flying Heinkel He 111 bombers (photo below). I became a member of the famous *'Griefen-Geschwader'*, I.Staffel; II Gruppe; KG 55. I was assigned to the Adjutant of the Group Commander, Oberleutnant Frick. With him I flew for 2 years, 81 combat missions, till the end of War

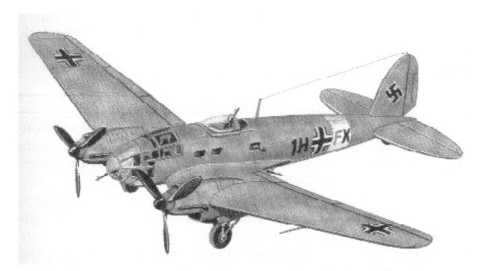

End of August we were assigned to the Eastern Front and flew to the Southern Sector. Few days later we were in combat. We were flying four missions a day, attacking troop positions, tanks, artillery, rocket launchers etc. On the first day in combat, we lost our Squadron Commander, when his plane blew up in mid-air. A bomb was stuck in his bomb bay after the drop. The two crews flying as wingmen were injured by the explosion.

Next day, our crew didn't do so well either. On the second mission of the first day in combat we also had the misfortune that one bomb got stuck in the bomb bay. As I went back to check on the bomb, I had mixed feelings.....it could blow up in my face at any minute. Between the bomb bays, I was short of oxygen because of the high altitude. Suddenly I heard shells hitting the plane! We were under attack by three Russian fighters. We took two cannon hits in the main spar of the right wing, one foot next to the fuel tank. Luckily I found the bomb safe and we returned to our base - so we were lucky to survive the first day in combat.

The damage to our bomber was serious and the wing had to be replaced. We regretted that we could not fly that day anymore. But we had a saying:
"Who knows what it is good for?"

Often it turned out to be our luck. In the following weeks, I accumulated sixteen combat missions.

It was early 1944 when Air Command had to regroup. We began training for night missions because Russian defenses had become too heavy in daytime. We Navigators had to learn astro-navigation. The pilots were training takeoffs and landings at night. One crew crashed during takeoff. We had to go pick them up. For the first time I could see what happened to air crews when they crashed. There were no survivors. The bomber had exploded on impact and only the tail section was in one piece. The pilot lay crushed under one of the engines. The radioman was still strapped into his seat. The third man we could find in the debris only after it got light.

We buried our comrades with full military honors in a small cemetery in a middle of a nowhere in Polish soil. More and more of us would follow as the war progressed.

The ones who crashed on takeoffs when one engine failed, we buried. But most of the crews never came back, missing in action and we didn't know what had happened to them. Even if they had bailed out and survived it, they were dead as well because the Russians were shooting all captured German bomber crews.

On April 20, 1944 I was promoted to the rank of Unteroffizier (Non-Commissioned Officer). I received also the **IRON CROSS 2nd CLASS** and the **BRONZE FLYING COMBAT BADGE** for completing 25 combat missions. It was for me a proud day when the Squadron Commander pinned the medal to my tunik in front of the Squadron.

On a daylight supply mission to the fortress Kovel in early spring 1944, one engine caught fire. It was on the 2nd mission of that day. I dropped the 2,500kg of supply bombs in a forest. We could blow out the fire by diving steeply. We made it back safely on one engine to the airfield *Baranowitshe*. The engine had to be replaced. Later we found out that a radioman from another crew was killed over the target. The night before, we had celebrated with him. It was always hard when we lost old comrades so suddenly.

The Luftwaffe Command began systematic strategic bombing missions of rail stations, supplying the front with war material in the Ukraine. Massive night attacks were carried out, with several Bomber Wings on *'Bomberstrom Ost"* (bomberstream east). We were attacking those train stations with great success, destroying about 2,000 rail cars each mission.

On these missions, twice we lost an engine and barely made it back to base. We landed on one engine, without damaging the plane. This required good pilot skills. All together, we had to come back home on one engine - four times.

Although our engines were replaced every 50 hours, sometimes they did not hold up that long. Flying a heavy bomber with one engine was always a nightmare. The running engine was pulling the plane to the side, which required heavy opposite rudder. The pilot didn't have the strength to hold the pressure alone for long. I and the Flight Engineer had to help him, sometimes for one hour. Then even we got tired and many times had to tie the rudder down with a string.

End of May 1944, our crew was transferred to a Pathfinder Group 9; Staffel III; Group of KG 4;' General Wever'. Pathfinders had the task of finding the target, lighting it out & mark it, for the following bomber wings. This was all new to us and we got some briefing.

On each mission, three Target Markers were assigned. I was chosen to fly as target Marker. This was a most difficult and responsible job. The marker had to be renewed four times during the attack. This kept me over the target for one hour. I flew at 3,000 meters through the heavy anti-aircraft defenses again and again. The bombers, flying at 5,000 meters, were aiming at our markers on the ground and at the same time, dropping their bombs right on top of us. The more accurate the markers were; the better was the bombers chances of hitting the target successfully.

Four weeks after leaving KG 55, our former Squadron had to fly a supply mission for the Army near Bobruisk. At low level they unexpectedly flew into a Russian flak barrage. Seven crews, the whole Squadron was lost. Had we not been transferred, we would have been among them. Such was the fate of war.

On one mission, 300 miles west from Moscow, the other two TM had engine trouble and had to return to base. So this time, 300 bombers of several wings were depending on my marksmanship. I had just put my marker in the center of the target, when we were attacked by a Russian night fighter. The search lights had caught us and he could see us well. He was only 100 meters away. But I outsmarted him by shooting two green flares into the sky. This was the Russian recognition signal for that night, which we always knew through our spies. The fighter turned away from us, thinking we were a Russian plane.

I put several more good markers on the target. The attack was a great success. For this, I received the **IRON CROSS FIRST CLASS** (previous page) and the **COMBAT BADGE** in **SILVER** for completing 60 missions.

Towards the end of 1944, we didn't fly bombing missions anymore. By this time, the Russians had taken Poland, Hungary and part of East Germany. There were many cauldrons and fortress cities, which we had to supply from the air.

In Spring 1945, I flew twelve missions to the fortress Budapest; six to Breslau. The last one of the War, supplying V. Panzer (5th Panzer) Division near Berlin. On the first mission to Budapest, I had just dropped the supply bombs when about 40 searchlights caught us in their beams. They were positioned on the surrounding hills. Flak was blasting us from all directions. Blinding light was in the cockpit. We went into a steep dive. The engines were screaming and all Hell was loose. About 400 meters over the roofs, we leveled off and raced away.

We returned to Budapest 3 more times that night, but the lights never caught us again because we were constantly changing our RPM.

A few weeks later, we had a similar experience when we flew a night attack on a bridge over the Danube, at Dunafoeldvar, Hungary. I had dropped the bombs and right after, we were caught by the searchlights. Heavy and medium flak was blasting us. So close that we could see the black puffs of smoke from the shells. A down swing got us in the cover of darkness again.

On our first mission to Breslau, we dropped the supplies at low level on the field. Suddenly, three Russian fighters attacked us from behind. One got very close, and our radioman fired two cannon rounds into his belly. He turned away steeply, diving towards the ground, probably shot down. After the second round, our gunner's cannon fell into his lap and he could shoot no more. The weapons guy had not secured the cannon properly. This mistake could have cost us our lives. Meanwhile, I could see the tracers all around us, as the other two fighters were making passes at us. I was kneeling on the floor of the cockpit, giving commands to my pilot, which way to turn to get away from the salvos. Diving and turning steeply about 400 meters above ground, we finally escaped.

We had numerous hits in the right engine and all over the fuselage - but we were still flying. This was my 75th combat mission. I will never forget it.

About 15 minutes later, we ran into German FLAK, which was shooting at us. Our Command had not reported that we would pass through there. Suddenly, I saw a big hole appear beside me in the wing. We were hit again, but still flying. Soon it got dark and we settled down for the one and one half hour flight to base. Heavy clouds came up and I could not see the ground anymore. I urged my pilot to go below the clouds so I could navigate by sight. He decided to stay up until the time was up. This was a mistake we had to regret.

When we let down through the cloud cover, we could see that the wind had carried us way off course, right into the Alps. We were in a valley with high mountain peaks on each side of us. We had to follow along the valley until we finally came out. We were already in Hungary. I set course to base and we landed at our field one hour late. Our comrades had already given up on us, thinking that we had been shot down that day.

The following missions to Breslau we flew only at night. We lost there, several more crews - three from our squadron. Two were shot down by FLAK; we witnessed one as they got hit. Their left engine burned and as the fire spread, the wing broke away. They went into a spiral and exploded on the ground.

From the other one we learned that the navigator crashed with the plane into the city. His parachute was caught on the tail. Only the pilot could bail out and save himself. He came back to our unit.

Another crew flew into a hill on the return flight. They came to us a few weeks before and had little experience. My crew had to go pick up their remains. At their funeral I was one of the pallbearers. As we strained under the heavy load, blood was oozing out of the casket on my hand.

Why did they have to die? Two weeks later, the War was over.

We flew our last mission of the War on April 28th, 1945 to the gates of Berlin. Our IV PanzerDivision was surrounded in a cauldron, 48 kilometers SE of Berlin and needed fuel desperately. They were holding off the attack of the 1st Bielorussian Army under General Zhokow. We had taken off from our base at Königgratz, Czechoslovakia. It was a clear night which made navigating much easier. My target was located in a vast forest along the swamps of the (river) Spree and to find it was like looking for a needle in a haystack. So I decided on a different approach. I chose for my first checkpoint, Lake Scharmutzelsee, the largest in the area, which was easy to find. From there I turned to a smaller Schwielocksee, and from there again to the smaller yet Kehrig-See which was very close to my target. From there, I followed a road along which the Panzers were waiting. As I approached, flares shot up in the sky and I dropped my load.

On the way back, I passed the city of Cottbus. My thoughts went to my parents. Here they had found shelter after escaping from Poland separately on January 18th, 1945 from the attacking Russian Army. Miraculously, after six weeks, they had found each other in the chaos.

The Eastern Front & the Western Front only Miles Apart

Underneath our bomber, an unusual sight in this War. Outlined by the burning fires, I could see the Eastern and Western Fronts simultaneously. Between them, a narrow strip of our homeland, for which our soldiers were still fighting.

In the last days of the war we were ordered to destroy all our planes on the ground. It was sheer confusion everywhere. We could have flown in them to the West, taking twenty people with us and surrender to the Americans. But, someone in our command made a stupid decision. Later it cost the lives of many of us in Russian captivity.

On 10th May we surrendered to the Russian Army. The war in Europe was over.

The crew of the Heinkel He 111 "Anton Kurfurst" (our call sign) had survived the war without a scratch. But later our Gunner, Uffz. Schultz and Flight Engineer, Uffz. Heinemann died in captivity. Our Radioman spent 18 months in Russia, and was released when he became gravely ill.

My pilot Oberleutnant Frick spent 4 years in captivity. He was our last Squadron Commander. Now we are the sole survivors. When I visited him a year ago he told me that shortly before the war ended, our crew had been recommended for the **German Cross in Gold** (below). This was one class below the **Ritterkreuz**, but by then, the war was over.

CHAPTER 3

Bombers are Supposed to Sink Submarines – but not their Own!

From Sharkhunters Member Bill Rooney

This is from an interview by USAAF veteran Bill Rooney with USAAF veteran James Giannatti, pilot of a B-18 bomber, covering an ASW mission on 13 July, 1942 that almost went very wrong - for the U. S. Navy!

Shortly after the War began and having survived the *'Battle of Borinquen'* I received orders to take my squadron (the 45th) to Aruba and set up operations to protect our oil tankers steaming toward the Panama Canal. Our B-18s were armed with .30 cal. machine guns and four depth charges that were fused to explode at a depth of 50 feet.

The mission proved to be quite frustrating. We knew that there were German submarines stalking the tankers because it was an all too familiar sight to see a column of black smoke on the horizon and find that another tanker had fallen victim to the Germans. It was not a pretty sight to see the flaming tankers wallowing in the water with many crewmen swimming for their lives in the flaming oil on the water's surface - or to see a lone lifeboat with only one man aboard who did not lift his face or wave when we flew 50 feet off to one side. I wanted to fight in the worst way! But where was the enemy? He was safely hidden beneath the water, licking his chops. I have never seen a more dedicated group of men than those of the 45th. They were determined to avenge this carnage.

Many of the bombers returned to base with fuel tanks registering close to empty. My anger reached a high point when an enemy sub sank a tanker almost beneath us on one of our patrols. This time we thought that at least we were able to fight back. We dropped our depth charges on a large cigar-shaped image (indistinct) just below the surface of the water. The roiled waters coughed up some debris and oil, but this was another ruse that the Germans employed.

> **EDITOR NOTE** - It is highly unlikely a German U-Boat would take the time and effort to go through such a ruse for an aircraft attack. This was normally done when destroyers with almost unlimited depth charges and plenty of time were above them and usually when the U-Boat was wounded. For an attack by aircraft, they would just go silent and deep but during the heat of battle, not all these facts come to light.

Shortly after this event, the 45th was moved to France Field in Panama from which we continued our patrol efforts. On a rainy morning in 1942 my crew and I departed in the trusty B-18 on another patrol. The only crewman I can remember was the Bombardier, Marshall *'Shorty'* Norton. Before departing, a senior officer briefed me as follows:

> 'In order to press a successful attack on an enemy sub, it was vital to do so without hesitation. The enemy sub could submerge in less than a minute. The best target would be on the surface or just beneath. Furthermore, a system of sanctuaries had been devised for friendly subs. Friendlies would be in these sanctuaries so it would be wise to stay away from those areas. Also, friendly subs would be identified by specific color markings on their decks. The American Flag would be flying at the stern. Identifying signal flares would be fired by friendly subs in recognition. Further, friendly subs will be submerged. If, for some reason, that is not possible, you will advise by radio.'

We departed and started our search, flying at about 500 feet weaving in and out between local rain squalls. As we circled a squall, lo and behold, just ahead of us, less than half a mile away, on the surface, was a long, cigar-shaped black sub.

In less than a wink, as we overtook the sub, it was evident that this sub was not friendly because it lacked color markings, there was no American

Flag, there were no flares, it wasn't in a sanctuary and I had received no message that an American sub was in the area. I immediately passed a command to open the bomb bay and to take battle positions for an attack. We dived to about 200 feet above the water. Our bomb run was at a 45 degree angle to the sub. *Shorty* Norton dropped his depth charges in a perfect strike. I wasn't able to see the bombs explode because I pulled up into a steep Chandelle, looking back at the sub over my shoulder. As we came around 180 degrees, I saw the sub rocking at a 45 degree angle in the midst of an inferno of boiling water. The nose gunner was training his .30 cal. machine gun eager to strafe the deck. I was elated! Now it was our turn to dump the Germans in the water.

Oops! My Error – So Sorry!

My elation quickly turned to chagrin when I saw an American Flag suddenly pop out at the stern! I immediately turned my radio to the Navy frequency, and I heard a torrent of expletives that made me fully understand what the phrase '*Cuss like a sailor*' really means.

I was thoroughly disgusted with myself. I can't recall the exact sequence of events after that. I apologized. I asked about casualties and damage. I advised the individual on the other end that I would report the incident and request an emergency destroyer come to the rescue immediately. Also, I advised that I would remain overhead as long as fuel would permit.

As I circled, I had worrisome thoughts. What would be my fate? Could I be court-martialled for aiding the enemy? How could I face my peers if Hitler wrote me a ***letter of commendation***? I dreaded the thought that I may have hurt or even killed my fellow Americans. It was obvious that the sub was badly damaged. It just seemed to be dead in the water.

I circled the sub as long as possible and then returned to France Field. The Base Commander, having been erroneously informed that I had sunk a German sub, had quickly assembled an Honor Guard to greet me. I walked up to the Commander who was beaming, and I told him:
   "*Sir, it was an American sub!*"

I have never seen a countenance change so fast in my life, nor have I ever seen an Honor Guard evaporate into thin air!

I learned the next day that the American sub that I had so flagrantly violated was en route to its home base after a hairy patrol in enemy waters near Japan. They thought they were in friendly waters and were home free. They were anticipating shore leave when they got into port at Norfolk, and this was to be nixed by some flyboy.

EDITOR NOTE - this is not an entirely accurate scenario. This sub was *S-16* and while she was indeed returning from patrol, she had never been in enemy waters nor even remotely near Japan. She was based at Coco Solo, Panama and all her war patrols, six of them, were conducted in the Caribbean. *S-16* was under command of Lieutenant Commander O. E. Hagberg for all six patrols. She was on her sixth and final patrol when attacked by this B-18 and unlike her previous patrols of two to three weeks, this one was only 5 days. *S-16* was soon decommissioned and returned to Key West where she was scuttled offshore. This was not because of any damage connected with this errant attack.

USS S-16

I received word that a crewman on board the sub observed our menacing approach and rushed to shoot the necessary identifying flares, but that the pin stuck and he used his teeth to pull it out. He lost several teeth in the process. I didn't sleep well that night and worried that I was destined to be hanged from the yardarm of some Navy ship.

My Commander talked to me shortly after the mishap. He informed me that I should have no trepidations. I had followed orders and deserved a letter of commendation. Furthermore, he said, the sub skipper should receive a letter or reprimand for not following orders. I felt somewhat relieved, but couldn't help feeling that I certainly wasn't helping out our effort to win the War.

I was later informed by the experts in ordnance that the reason the sub was not sunk even though the bombs were placed perfectly was because of the fusing. Fifty feet was beyond the lethal radius. If the fuses were set at 25 feet, it would have been curtains for the sub. Therefore, the near miss was in a vertical direction instead of horizontal. *Shorty* Norton was too good a bombardier to miss a shot like that.

It was comforting to learn later that there were no serious injuries suffered aboard the sub. For the sailor who pulled out those signal flare pins with his teeth, I can see in my mind's eye the look of disbelief of some Navy dentist when he asked - *'How **did** you get those teeth knocked out?'*

The incident as remembered by the **NAVY** . . .

From **SubRonThree** at Coco Solo, a report was filed which said:
'An investigation is being made by Commander Panama Sea Frontier of the bombing of *S-16* by friendly planes. From reports received to date, the bombing appears to be the result of a series of mistakes, none of which were made by the *S-16*. Commander SubRonThree has made certain recommendations to Commander Panama Sea Frontier which should prevent future occurrences. A report of this incident is being forwarded to Commander Submarines, Atlantic Fleet. The damage appears to be minor and does not warrant docking the vessel prior to her scheduled overhaul period.'

CHAPTER 4

Reward Offered for the Black Devil

This piece is written by Sharkhunters Member Manfred Roeder about Sharkhunters Member Erich Hartmann, the top scoring fighter pilot ever in history. Three hundred fifty two enemy planes fell from his onslaught. No fighter pilot ever came close.

Manfred (left) with Cooper

Hartmann

In memory of the top fighter *ACE* of all time; **Col. Erich Hartmann**.

10,000 Rubles were set on his head, the *Black Devil* - the most successful fighter pilot of the world, Erich Hartmann. He died September 21 (1993) with 71 years of age. *'BILD'*, the largest paper in Germany, carried a short notice with a negative slant. Not much else was in the press. With 352 air victories he was not only the **ACE** of all **ACES**, but also a man of noble character, a hero for the youth.

The Russians feared his Me 109 with the black nozzle (therefore the *Black Devil*) so much that they went out of his way. For Hartmann had developed a fighting technique which hardly ever failed. He always came as a surprise, went straight at the enemy at very close distance, sometimes 30 yards, before he opened fire. The result was always devastating. He never engaged in curving battles. Once he shot down three heavily armoured Russian battle planes in a row and used only 120 rounds. In his most spectacular action, he downed four fighter bombers with only one cone of fire. When the first bomber exploded the other three dived in a panic and hit the ground. His record day was in March 1944 when he shot down ten planes.

Hartmann was a daredevil but no ambitious egotist. He did not regard his air victories as his greatest fame but the fact that he never lost a comrade that was attached to him in flight. (Fighter planes were always flying by two, protecting each other). His younger, less experienced comrades he always brought home safely. In spite of his courage, he was never reckless. If he could not attack from a good position he just left it. And he also developed a technique of defense and was never wounded.

But like most pilots, he had several emergency landings. In one case he saw a certain German army truck approaching, but the two men jumped off were Russians who took him prisoner. Hartmann behaved like being heavily wounded and was loaded on the truck. Suddenly he pushed his guard over and jumped off, running into the field. They shot and shouted after him but he made it back to the German lines.

Openness and directness were part of his character. When he was 17 he fell in love with the 15 year old Ursula Paetsch. In order to introduce himself he raced toward her on a bicycle when she was just walking home from school. In front of her he came to a screaming halt, dropped his bike and, blushing said: '*My name is Erich Hartmann.*' It was the beginning of a love that lasted to the very end, enduring all hardships and temptations.

Hartmann was three times received by Hitler. When he was decorated with the **OAK LEAVES** of the **KNIGHTS CROSS**; again with **SWORDS**; and the third time when he received the **DIAMONDS**. The first time he arrived at the Berghof in an elated spirit because of the drinks he had been offered in the train. He took the Führer's hat from the rack to try it on. The aide was shocked. Hartmann looked and often behaved like a schoolboy and usually was called '*BUBI*'. When he came to be decorated with the **DIAMONDS**, he was asked to remove his pistol as was the directive after the attempt of the 20th of July 1944. He refused and said to the aide:

'Tell the Führer that I do not want his **DIAMONDS** if he has no confidence in his fighting officers.'

He could keep his pistol and gave Hitler an unvarnished picture of the situation at the front.

Before the end of the War, he married his Usch during a three weeks furlough. But after one week, he said:

'I have no right to be happy in your arms, Usch, while my comrades are in battle. I have to go back.'

Usch was in tears but she understood. New Year 1945 he came again for a few days and they did not know that it was the last time for more than eleven years. On the last day of the War he shot down his 352nd plane.

His general ordered him to fly to Dortmund and turn himself over to the British to avoid revenge of the Russians, for Hartmann had fought almost entirely at the Eastern Front. It would have saved him ten horrible years. He stayed, was arrested by an American unit and then turned over to the Russians. What then happened to others in his group he could never forget for the rest of his life. Rape and murder at gunpoint, and suicides during the whole night - nobody could come to their help.

Hartmann was 23 years, just promoted to Major, decorated with the highest order which only 27 soldiers received during the War. He was the most famous fighter pilot in history. But all of this did not count any more. Now he grew up to his full greatness - a real man. Many gave up or even turned to be traitors, including high officers. Hartmann stood like a rock and never wavered. For more than ten years he fought the NKVD, the Soviet secret police against all odds.

The Russians tried to win him as a collaborator or for the new German Communist Luftwaffe. He steadfastly refused. Each time he was thrown into a bunker for many weeks - a dark dungeon with no heat, no blankets -

nothing. At one point the NKVD officer lost his temper and beat Hartmann with a stick. This was too much. Hartmann grabbed a chair and crashed it down on the interrogator. Then he called the guard outside, expecting to be shot or beaten to death, but nothing happened. Three days later the same officer called him, offered him vodka and bread, and apologized for the beating.

Many times he went on hunger strike. He was forced to eat. They wanted him alive. Finally he was sentenced as a war criminal to 25 years hard labor because his bullets that missed enemy planes might have fallen down and killed civilians on the ground....Russian logic. Hartmann's answer:
 'Shoot me! I am not afraid of death.'

When his wife read about this in the paper her mother said:
 *'Erich will be over 60 when he returns home.
   How can you bear that?'*

 'If they keep him until he is 70, I will wait for him.'
was Usch's answer. It was this unwavering love that kept Hartmann alive. The NKVD almost killed him when they touched on that secret. They told him they had the power to cut off the heads of his wife and son and bring them to him on a platter if he would not cooperate; or they waved five letters from his wife before his eyes and would not give them to him.

He broke down in his dark bunker and wept like a child. He told himself:
 'Erich, you must not give up. Fight your worst enemy-hunger. You must not die. You must live for Usch and your son.'

He broke off his hunger strike but continued fighting. As a war criminal he was transferred to a special camp where they had to work like slaves. Hartmann refused:
 'I am not a criminal but a German officer and according to the Geneva Convention, I am not obligated to work.'

Nobody cares about any convention and nobody will notice your death, he was told. He was put back into the bunker again and tortured. This had the effect of a match in a power keg. With a cry of revenge, a hundred prisoners attacked the guards, liberated all incarcerated men including Russian political prisoners, who immediately fled out of the camp, encouraged by the population. But when some of the Germans wanted to follow, Hartmann stopped them:

'Don't run away. They will shoot you like dogs. You have no chance. Let us fight for better conditions in the camp.'

And he telephoned the general in the headquarters and talked to him in Russian. A committee from Moscow was ordered, but Hartmann was transferred again and isolated.

It was the last camp with the most famous prisoners. Hartmann's arrival gave them new hope which they had lost completely. His name was well known, not for his courage in the War but for his courage afterwards, his fight against the secret police. When the car with Erich stopped in a cloud of dust, all inmates came rushing forward and hailed him with loud applause. Here came the **BLOND KNIGHT** - slim, tattered, dirty - but unbroken, proud and radiant with hope. He had a feeling that their time in captivity was almost over and he was right. In Nov. 1955, they were released after Adenauer had made agreements with Kruschev. In those years his father had died; so had his little son, whom he had never seen.

Ray Toliver

The happiest days the Hartmanns spent were in America where he had to test new fighter planes, and was treated as the most famous pilot and good comrade and where they experienced the best of hospitality for which the Americans are second to none, which I can confirm myself.

It is noteworthy that the story of Hartmann's life was written by two American authors, (Sharkhunters Member) Ray Toliver and Constable, and it became the Book of the Month in America. In Germany, Hartmann is almost unknown............

CHAPTER 5

A Mystery Solved

Captain William Barnard (USN Retired) sends this first-person memory of his time in the war after he saw a copy of the **KTB** Magazine of Sharkhunters from his friend and Sharkhunters Member John Carlin. He writes:

Carlin was my Plane Captain (crew chief) or in my plane crew over relatively long period of WWII which took us sub hunting from the Iceland/Newfoundland area to the most southern part of Brazil with a lot of stops such as river mouths and islands and other odd places that seaplanes could get in and out of. We covered a large part of the Atlantic Ocean and tried to be always where the German sub activity was the heaviest. I have always found John to be a very modest man, thus it didn't surprise me to see that he had not mentioned several things about himself in connection with the list of subs sunk by our Squadron. By the way, he also did not mention subs attacked, wounded, unknown damage etc. nor did he say anything about the two hundred eighty five shipwrecked (torpedoed) sailors that the Squadron rescued during that period

John participated in the sinking of *U-128*, Skippered by Steinert (photo next page). From that boat was taken (if my memory is correct) fifty eight prisoners. A goodly number of these German submariners were saved because we dropped them liferafts when the sub was in a sinking position. John Carlin was promoted to Chief Petty Officer while we were still in the air for his part in this sinking. With this promotion, he became the youngest Chief Petty Officer in the Navy at age 20. He was further decorated by the Secretary of the Navy in the name of the President with the *AIR MEDAL* which at that time was a prestigious decoration.

The End of *U-128*

John was also my Plane Captain on February 24, 1943 when we made a *'mystery attack'* on another submarine. This submarine, to the best of my knowledge, has never been identified and maybe that would be a good research project for either your German or Italian Members. The attack occurred on 24 February, 1943 off the coast of Natal, Brazil.

We found this sub while it was in the process of sinking a cargo vessel of about 10,000 tons with a Spanish name and flying a Spanish flag. In fact, we determined the location the sub by following two torpedo wakes from the ship to the sub, which was lying just below the surface in almost crystal clear water. We were on a mission to locate and identify a reported ship out of Argentina which was supposedly hauling contraband gold and German spies out of the country. Our mission was to herd this ship into the nearest port if the identification was confirmed. We had made a low run on the ship, picked off its name and nationality, and climbed back to about 1,500 feet to make our report make to the base and receive instructions on further action at the time the ship was torpedoed. We immediately initiated an attack run on the sub with it in sight submerged.

EDITOR NOTE – Axis ships and submarines were indeed making clandestine runs to and from Argentina from 1938 until 1947 and possibly even later. Information on these actions can be found in our book "*Escape from the Bunker*" which is available from Sharkhunters.

When within about half a mile of the sub with the plane in attack configuration, at attack speed and altitude, the sub surfaced and began firing at us. The first fire came from a '*bandstand*' aft and seemed to be remotely controlled. Immediately thereafter the bow gun was manned and began firing. Due to faulty machine gun parts which had been installed in all ten of our .50cal the night before, we were unable to reply with any gunfire and thus unable to sweep the decks or protect ourselves. We continued our run and dropped six five-hundred pound depth charges.

This was a full deflection run with the sub underway and the depth charges fell short, except that the last one or two were close enough to deluge the decks of the sub with water. To shorten it - the sub stayed on the surface for about one and a half hours and seemed to be trying to dive.

Without the ability to attack, we tried to stay out of range of his larger deck gun and kept reporting our position in order to get any other American forces on the scene. He managed to dive before any arrived.

We had suffered no damage at all except one strut of the starboard wingtip float shot in two and the 26 foot-long float dangling by one strut and giving us a fit in the control department. We managed to twist it off through flight maneuvering. When we got back to base, we found that we had one hundred fifty six holes in the aircraft with some of them going right through the engine nacelles but not hitting any vital parts.

I was never given any kind of an evaluation for this account. The common knowledge and our ASW '*Grapevine*' told us that this was the first sub that had surfaced and engaged an attacking airplane and that it was the first of a series of new subs that had the remote control

'*BANDSTAND*' machine gun set up on the stern. These same rumors told us that it was an Italian submarine.

This sort of embarrassed me as at that time we didn't think of the Italian Navy as any kind of threat. Our official Squadron history that was made available after the classified label was taken off it just shows that the attack was made and has no assessment or evaluation at all on it. In our estimation, the sub was surely damaged, probably the diving planes jammed or it would have submerged long before it did in order to avoid any other potential attacks. We have never had any confirmation as to whether or not it was Italian and in all of the intelligence reports that I have seen since then having to do with the ASW activities in the Atlantic. I have never seen any reference to this attack.

We saw no boats being put over the side from the torpedoed ship and we saw no survivors in the water after the ship was sunk. It appeared to us that the ship sunk within a very few minutes after it was torpedoed. I would appreciate any comments on this attack from either you or any of your historically inclined Members.

The Mystery Solved

The submarine was indeed Italian - it was **BARBARIGO** and the Skipper was Captain Roberto Rigoli. The ship that was attacked was the Spanish steamer **MONTE IGUELDO** of 3,453 tons. Rigoli earned the '**MEDAGLIO D'ARGENTO**' or the **SILVER MEDAL**, Italy's second highest award. Earlier in the War, while in command of **PLATINO**, he sank the **NARKUNDA**, a 16,632 ton British transport in the Mediterranean. It was the largest ship sunk by an Italian submarine in the Mediterranean during WW II. Rigoli ultimately sank more than 32,000 tons of Allied shipping.

CHAPTER 6

The First Trans-Atlantic Flight

This flight was the NC-4, the idea conceived in August, 1917. Rear Admiral David W. Taylor determined that for antisubmarine work the Navy needed a large, sea-based patrol bomber capable of flying directly to the war in Europe, instead of taking up space aboard ship. Glenn H. Curtiss, head of the Curtiss Aeroplane and Motor Company was called in as design consultant.

In January 1918, the Navy awarded Curtiss a contract for four flying boats. The parts were manufactured at various sites and then assembled at the Curtiss plant at Garden City, Long Island, New York. Only nine months after award of contract on October 4, 1918, the NC-1 (Navy-Curtiss-1) with Cmdr. H.C. Richardson and Lt. D. McCulloch at the controls, rose from Jamaica Bay on her first flight.

A month later, World War One ended, and the need for these flying boats was no longer seen as critical. However, it had been proposed that these NC boats attempt a trans-Atlantic flight before the summer of 1919. After studying several routes, it was found that the NC did not have sufficient range to fly nonstop from Newfoundland to Ireland or England. Therefore they would fly via the Azores and Portugal. Plans were approved on February 4.

The NC-1 was built as a tri-motor, and it was calculated that better performance could be achieved with 4 engines, so the NC-2 was modified with four engines in tandem pairs. This arrangement was not found to be efficient. On the NC-3 and NC-4, there were four engines, but the arrangement was three tractor engines and one pusher engine mounted in tandem over the hull centerline. NC-1 was then converted to this configuration.

NC-2 became "spare parts" to keep NC-1 flying following damage by a storm on March 27, and a hangar fire on May 5.

On May 8, 1919 NC-1, NC-3 and NC-4 took off from Rockaway for Halifax, Nova Scotia, beginning their Trans-Atlantic flight. They were under command of John Towers, commander and navigator of NC-3.

NC-4's center engine failed off Cape Cod, so she landed at sea and taxied into the Naval Air Station at Chatham, Massachusetts. NC-3 and NC-1 arrived at Halifax with serious cracks in their propellers which were replaced the next day.

On May 10 NC-1 and NC-3 continued their flight to Trepassey, Newfoundland, the start of their long journey. At Trepassey all was ready. There were 21 destroyers on station at 50-mile intervals between Cape Race, Newfoundland and Corvo, the westernmost of the Azores Islands. This was considered a safety precaution as in 1919 this kind of navigation, much less reliable communication were not the science they are today.

Repairs had been completed on NC-4, and she waited for clear weather to make the jump to Trepassey. She arrived on the 15th, the date the NC-1 and NC-3 were scheduled to leave.

NC-1 and NC-3, however, were overloaded with fuel and could not take off; in addition, the weather report for the 16th looked even more favorable. They waited and on Friday evening, May 16, the three boats flew into the gathering darkness over the Atlantic. They chose an evening takeoff so they could arrive in the Azores in daylight.

At dawn, sunrise was closely followed by fog. NC-3 spotted a ship on the horizon, took it to be one of the destroyers, and altered course accordingly. It was the cruiser **MARBLEHEAD** returning from Europe. This error took NC-3 far off course, and she had to land to take a navigation sight. The seas were high, and the impact of landing collapsed the struts supporting the centerline engines. NC-3 could only operate as a surface craft from that point.

NC-1 had similar problems, but was able to land without incident. However she could not take off again through the 12 foot waves. She would be lucky to survive the swells.

NC-4 had also run out of guiding destroyers and was also virtually lost. The radio officer, however, was able to pick up radio bearings and weather information from the destroyers, which were in fact still below although hidden by fog and clouds. After more than fifteen hours flying, NC-4's pilot was assured that he was very near the Azores. In a break in the fog Flores was spotted as a checkpoint. With the fog closing in again, Read landed NC-4 in the harbor of Horta shortly before noon.

The other ships: NC-1's crew was rescued by the Greek freighter ***IONIA***. However the attempts to salvage NC-1 were thwarted by heavy seas. She sank three days later. NC-3 sailed into the harbor of Ponta Delgada on the island on Sao Miguel in the eastern Azores on May 19.

Weather and engine trouble delayed NC-3's next leg of the journey for a week. She took off at 0818 hours on Tuesday, May 27 for Lisbon, again with a chain of destroyers between the islands and the city. At 1939 hours the Cabo da Roca lighthouse, the westernmost point in Europe had been spotted, and minutes later NC-4 roared over, turning southward toward the Tagus estuary and Lisbon.

Lieutenant Commander A. C. Read, commander of NC-4 said that moment was *"perhaps the biggest thrill of the whole trip"*. At 2001 hours on May 27, 1991, NC-4 landed in the Tagus estuary. Two days later NC-4 was to continue her flight to Plymouth, England, however she was forced down by double engine trouble. Although the difficulties were minor, the window for a daylight landing had been lost. Therefore she spent the night at El Ferrol, Spain, and on May 30, flew to Plymouth, landing there in the early afternoon.

CHAPTER 7

A Secret Kept

More great historic input from Sharkhunters Member Bill Rooney.

Security leaks. Poor Jimmy. Poor Ronnie, for that matter. Only a short time ago, they were reporting being *"up their kiesters in security leaks"*. Their trouble - as well as all of Washington and the world - is that they are unaware of *Rooney's Law #1*. This natural law could be characterized as Murphy's Law of the Secret, for *Rooney's Law #1* reads:
There is no such thing as a secret if someone else really wants to know.

This law operates in politics, business, warfare and society. It has been validated in history as well as in modern times. It was crystallized in Kharagpur, India during World War II (1944). It happened this way:

That night I had caught the duty as Charge of Quarters in the adjutant's office of the 20th Bomber Command. A group of us *Rear Rank Rudy's* who had been given authority to handle top secret documents were delegated this assignment in rotation. About supper time, one of the most startling messages to come into the Bomber Command was received and thrust at me by some Signal Corps officer. This cage-rattler carried across the top the usual **Top Secret** stamp (highest level of secrecy) and also carried a four "**Z**" stamp (highest speed of transmission). Moreover, it was from the War Department, rather than from an Air Corps Headquarters.

Holding the message with as steady a hand as I could muster, I read in it that General Curtis E. LeMay, the Bomber Command CO, was therewith ordered from India to the Marianas. I quickly took the hot potato down to the General's mess and got his aide's signature thereon, thus divesting myself of any further responsibility for it.

The next morning I returned to my usual desk duty. No sooner had I seated myself than one of our sergeants eased up to me and said, *"Jeezus, Captain, how about that."* He had not been on duty the previous night, nor even in the headquarters building, yet he knew the contents of the Top Secret message. He also knew that, by reason of my having had CQ duty, I knew what he was talking about. There was born *Rooney's Law #1*.

It seems somewhat strange, with all of the history which documents the inability of one holder of a secret to keep that secret out of the hands of someone who wants it, that we continue to do battle to protect the leakage.

Certainly, it is in wartime that the highest level of energy is expended to preserve secrecy. Yet, the British cracking of the German *"Ultra"* code in World War Two made it possible for the Allies to read German secrets almost as if they were being published in the *Frankfurter Zeitung*.

Our cryptographic intelligence sources had done the same with the Japanese *"Magic"* code. Using intelligence thus gained, we effectively turned back the Japanese at Midway and at Coral Sea. In addition, our reading of *"Magic"* provided us with a host of Japanese secrets from before the start of the war until its conclusion.

Both the Germans and Japanese thought their cipher systems were uncrackable. In the case of the Germans, the British were reading German messages with the same acumen in 1916 as they were in 1940.

As related in Barbara Tuchman's book *The Zimmerman Telegram*, a German cruiser was shattered in a battle with the British Navy in World War One. The German skipper, in order to forestall his code books from falling into enemy hands, encased them in a lead box, which he gave to a seaman with orders to set out from the ship in a small boat and get a distance from the ship before dropping the books overboard, precluding their being found in the sunken wreckage of his ship. However, the sailor was killed on his mission, and his body was pulled from the water by the British. He still clasped the lead-encased code books in his arms. Using this information to augment what they already had, the British were able to decode the famous telegram from the German foreign secretary,

Zimmerman, to his ambassador in America. It brought about the entry of the United States into World War One.

Today, the National Security Agency probably has computers decoding other computer encoded messages so that we, and everyone else - is reading each other's mail as if it were on postcards.

Probably the two most highly classified secret projects of World War II were the *Manhattan Project* (atomic bomb)and the *Matterhorn Project* (B-29). So secret was the *Matterhorn* Project, that even the name was hardly used. In 1943, our squadron, based at Pratt, Kansas, was the first to be assigned a B-29 combat aircraft. However, I doubt if I even heard the *Matterhorn* Project mentioned as many as a half-dozen times. And yet, if ever there were a security sieve, the *Matterhorn* Project was it.

Early on in the construction of the B-29's, the primary factory for their manufacture was the Boeing plant in Wichita, Kansas. Combat crews from squadron who were sent there for duty and to ferry planes back to our base, reported that anyone sitting in a car on a road skirting the plant could, unmolested, count the number of planes coming off the production lines. To assist any spy should he be vision-impaired, the Boeing plant had undertaken a morale-boosting gesture. They rang a giant bell every time a new plane came off the line. It wasn't until one of the captains in our outfit, who had been sufficiently frightened, or angered, by threats to us over any breach of security we might commit, called this security gaff to the attention of authorities, and it was stopped.

No matter. When the first contingent of B-29's landed at our four bases in India in 1943, the **Tokyo Rose** of Burma was on the airwaves welcoming the B-29's to India. As if this wasn't enough, the Japanese radio welcomed the planes by number and included mention of some of the crew members by name. To some extent, their information was faulty. Some of the crew assignments were garbled.

On December 14, 1944, on a combat mission to Rangoon, four or our planes were destroyed in mid-air. Approximately forty-four men were in the four aircraft. Of these about twenty-eight survived. All were taken prisoner by the Japanese and held in an infamous prison camp in Rangoon.

Since the B-29 was an instrument of terror to the Japanese, interrogators set about questioning these prisoners mercilessly. One of the Japanese interrogators (who had attended Washington State, he told his prisoners) used as his reference for questioning a copy of the November issue of *Air Force Magazine*, which contained one of the first openly published articles on the B-29. And this was an issue the crew members themselves had not yet seen.

As to the *Manhattan* Project, the extent to which the Germans might have penetrated the project is not generally known. Interestingly, the FBI had turned a German agent named Walter Koehler into a double agent - or so they thought. In truth, while Koehler was housed in an FBI hideout on Long Island from the summer of 1942 until the end of the war, and while he was supposedly sending to Germany FBI-controlled messages, it was learned after the war that he was, at the same time, sending out intelligence of the real kind over a transmitter in Rochester, New York.

Meanwhile, as early as November 12, 1940, messages were being sent to Germany from the US by one Alfred Hohlhaus, telling his handlers in Germany about US production of helium gas. In Farago's book, *The Game of the Foxes*, Hohlhaus us quoted as reporting to Germany that this helium production "could be connected with some significant development in nuclear physics."

A friend, writing about the business of secrecy surrounding the *Manhattan* Project, noted that our efforts at secrecy were directed not so much at protecting how much we knew at that time about atomic energy, but to forestall the enemy from knowing how little we knew. Much of what we did know early on was common scientific knowledge, yet it does jolt one in retrospect to recall the William L. Laurence, New York Times science editor, in the **Saturday Evening Post** issues of May 5 and September 7, 1940, wrote about *"the utilization of atomic energy."* He told about the substance U235, and described its power in TNT equivalency.

As for the Japanese penetration of the secrets of the *Manhattan* Project, information just recently obtained shows that they had set up a joint venture with Spain to locate agents in the US to find out what progress was being made in this country on the development of an atomic bomb.

Japanese efforts to create an atomic bomb were frustrated, it is reported, when some atomic-bomb making material being transported from Germany to Japan via submarine was lost when the sub was sunk.

EDITOR NOTE – Actually, several U-Boats were bound for Japan with uranium aboard. All were sunk except for *U-234* and that boat surrendered to the US when Germany surrendered. The Skipper of that boats as well as the I.W.O., the Cargo Officer and the Chief Radioman were all Sharkhunters Members.

US Navy Checking *U-234* in Portsmouth, NH

The written word was turned into cyphers for the purpose of concealment as early as the 14th century. Cyphering and decoding skills reached an interesting point in Vienna in the 1700's. Bags of mail intended for the embassies of Europe passed through Vienna. Mail brought into one Vienna black chamber at 7:00am was read, copied, decoded if such was needed, and put back into the mail by 2:00pm. Wax seals, thought to protect the security of the letters, were skillfully melted and replaced.

People have been trying to keep secrets since the beginning of time - and failing. First was the whispered secret carried by courier. A bit of torture applied to the courier was sufficient to extract the information. Tapping into the telegraph line when Morse's invention came of age removed an opportunity for secrecy there. And when Marconi's invention of the radio made possible the casting of messages across the airwaves, the deciphering of such messages has brought us up to the present.

The root of the problem of maintaining secrecy may be expressed in the cliché *"knowledge is power"*. The crafty one who has the knowledge that is secret seeks ways in which to profit from it. The ordinary secret-holder is solely an intermediary. He can gain satisfaction from possessing the secret only by giving it away, thus experiencing that yeasty sense of power that comes with having possession of a secret. It doesn't matter if it is a secret of national importance or a piece of neighborhood gossip, the thrill is there, however brief or tenuous.

Rooney's Law #1 still applies, and will continue to apply so long as someone has information someone else wants, or, so long as someone is privy to a secret that will provide the satisfaction of disposing of it either by selling it or giving it away.

CHAPTER 8

'FOO FIGHTERS II'

More strange sightings occurred toward the end of World War II in the skies over Europe and the Pacific. The Allies believed the Axis was developing a new secret weapon....and the Axis powers believed the same of the Allies. But what were they really? Secret weapons? Ball lightning? Energy fluctuations in the atmosphere reacting to the aircraft themselves? Or what? They were certainly, and by definition *UFO's* - not (necessarily) flying saucers - but *UNIDENTIFIED FLYING OBJECTS*.

Sharkhunters Members Baron Georg von Zirk and Green Beret Major Lou Mari continue with their observations.

George von Zirk flew with the Luftwaffe, and he tells us the following:

The article *"Foo Fighters"* was interesting to me. I had experienced an UFO, when I was flying a night combat mission in summer 1944. The place was the Middle Sector of the Russian Front.

We were en route to a target, I don't remember which any more. As always, I was lying in the front section of the cockpit, navigating. Suddenly a flying object overtook us from behind. It was on the same course as we. It passed as about 200 meters underneath, at a speed of a cannon shell. In the dark I could see only a large ball of fire, moving horizontally. It got out of sight in about 5 seconds. We were flying at an altitude of about 3,000 m.

I don't think that it was a VI rocket, because as far as I know, we used them only at the Western Front.

And, again thanks to Green Beret Major Lou Mari who references a book entitled *Intercept but Don't Shoot*, the *"Ball Lightning"* automatic fighter' was discussed.

Lou indicates that the article indicates that G. Werke built a symmetrical, circular aircraft, with direct gyroscope stabilization and hypercombustible fuel in a total reaction turbine, which also had jam-free radio control and infra red search. This craft was called the *Feuerball*.

An earlier device which actually had one mission, according to the article was the *Kugelblitz* (ball lightning) that had an electrostatic firing device, and was in essence the first "jet-lift" aircraft. The *Kugelblitz* was "destroyed by technical detachments of retreating SS troops", and nothing has ever been revealed.

These devices, according to the article, particularly the *Kugelblitz*, is the second authentic precursor of what we know today as flying saucers.

Okay, now for a third course on this fascinating topic: Timothy Good's *Above Top Secret - the Worldwide UFO Cover-Up*. According to his material, British intelligence set up an organization in 1943 to investigate the sightings of small, probably remote-controlled devices that were being reported by Allied air crews. These *"Foo fighters"* never engaged in hostile actions, but many air crews were convinced that the weapons were psychological.

This organization had its counterpart in Germany, called the *Sonder Büro #13* - code named *Operation Uranus*.

Not to be left out, the American US 8th Army also investigated the sightings, but with no conclusions. They were back to St. Elmo's Fire, ball lightning, and combat fatigue. And this was just in Europe.

Sightings of Foo-fighters (or something lumped under that catch-all name) also occurred in the Pacific. The crew of a B-29 bomber on its way from Ceylon, bombing Palembang, Sumatra had a sighting of an object keeping pace with them about 500 yards off the starboard wing; it was apparently spherical, 5-6 feet in diameter, bright red/orange, and seemed to vibrate.

The object followed the bomber's evasive maneuvering, and kept pace with it for approximately 8 minutes. When it departed, it made an abrupt 90 degree turn and accelerated rapidly, disappearing into the clouds. There was a detailed report on the sighting filed with Intelligence when the crew returned to their base.

Did the Luftwaffe Copy a Saucer?

Did the U.S. Air Force Copy from That?

CHAPTER 9

By a Pubic Hair......

Double ACE Sharkhunters Member Bob Goebel remembers air combat in World War Two.

Walt would have been aghast at the title, but it was true. He came that close to buying the farm. I had known Walt since our first days at Pre-flight when all the eager young men came together, not with stars, but silver wings in their eyes. Most, myself included, knew little more about flying than that the propeller end went first. Not so with Walt. Back in St. Louis, he was what was known as an airport rat, spending all his free time washing airplanes or doing odd jobs for flying time, or just hanging out. I think that he had 100+ hours when he arrived at the San Antonio Aviation Cadet Center, so he was viewed as someone to be sought out and listened to by the rest of us. And he continued his military flying career in the same vein after winning his wings, becoming in the process, a crackerjack fighter pilot.

We stuck together after graduation, through a tour in Panama in P-39's and then up in Italy in Mustangs in the same outfit, the 308th Squadron of the 31st Fighter Group. His mild manners and soft speech belied his fiery aggressiveness in aerial combat. After one mission to Wiener Neustadt, he told me, with an embarrassed laugh, what had happened.

The squadron had gotten into it with some Fw-190s. Walt latched onto one which had promptly led him into a vertical dive at full throttle. They accelerated very rapidly and when Walt got a few hits on his adversary, they were going so fast that the 190 just disintegrated in the air.

Walt was not exactly sure what happened to him thereafter, other than the stick was doing some things he had never felt before and he was just a passenger in that machine. He did get the throttle pulled back and as the aircraft got into the denser air of lower altitude and slowed down, he regained control. When he got it straight and level he was aware of the fact that the machine was not behaving right, but since it WAS flying and he had control of it, he decided to continue back to his base.

Welcome to 'Compressibility'

After he got it on the ground and we all got a look at it, it was quite apparent why it *"flew funny"*. The skin on the wings was badly wrinkled, suggesting some serious structural damage within. But what really looked strange was the view from the tail looking forward. The fuselage had a slight twist to it, which caused the tail to angle sideways instead of pointing straight up. The horizontal was equally offset. It was a matter of speculation what happened to Walt's wingman, he never made it back.

Walt did sneak the clock and altimeter out of **"*Miss Mini*"** before they hauled it off to the bone yard for salvage. We didn't know anything about compressibility or *Mach* in those days of innocence and happy ignorance, but we knew intuitively that he came within a fraction of an inch of pulling that plane apart. All of us, but especially Walt, took it all in stride and he got on with the job on succeeding missions with a new aircraft.

"A miss is as good as a mile."

(Walt Goehausen finished his tour with 10 victories and after the war, flew for PanAm for 36 years before retirement. In January of 1995 he finally lost a battle; to cancer.)

CHAPTER 10
Luftwaffe Memories I
Secret Weapons

Sharkhunters Member Rolf Zydek tells about it.

Much has been written and may be much even more speculated about Germany's secret weapons of WW II. This story about Luftwaffe Memories will deal with the "real thing" on Germany's wonder weapons.

The very first guided - missile attack in history was launched on August 25, 1943.

That afternoon twelve Dornier Do - 217's from II. Group KG 100 attacked Royal Navy escort vessels off the northwestern tip of Spain with glider bombs. Many of the missiles failed to function properly and only minor damage was caused to one of the corvettes.

However, in a more successful attach three days later the corvette *"EGRET"* was sunk and the destroyer *"ATHABASKAN"* was damaged.

One of the leading minds behind these attacks was Major Bernhard Jope of KG 100. And it was Jope's unit - III./KG 100 - which executed the first real success/attack with glider bombs; i.e. missile guided bombs.

FRITZ X in action

Early on the morning of September 9, 1943 the Italian battle fleet set sail from La Spezia for its final sortie. It was bound for Malta to surrender under the terms of the armistice which came to affect that day.

As the ships neared the narrow straits which separate Corsica and Sardinia, Major Jope personally leading a flight formation of eleven Dornier Do - 217K attacking that specific fleet which had only the previous day been their allies.

The bombers were armed with two FRITZ X guided bombs/missiles each. FRITZ X is a radio controlled flying bomb with fuselage, wings and tail rudder, and it could carry a warhead of about 500 lbs.

Now back to Major Jope and his flight of Dorniers Do 217 K's attacking the Italian fleet.

Two of the guided bombs struck the flagship *ROMA*, a modern 42,000 ton battleship. One hit near the aft mast penetrated the deck armor and damaged the starboard steam turbines heavily, reducing the ships speed to a mere 16 knots. A few minutes later *ROMA* (photo above) was again hit on the port side near the main bridge, thus bringing the remaining turbines to a standstill. Fierce fires inside the ship reached the ammunition bunkers after 20 minutes and the magazine exploded violently. **ROMA** broke into two parts, folded up like a jackknife, and sank minutes later with most of her crew.

Shortly after the attack on **ROMA**, her sistership **ITALIA** was also hit by a lone FRITZ X on the bow. The battleship suffered some damage and shipped 800 tons of water, but was able to reach Malta under her own steam.

On the same day as the Italian fleet sailed, Allied forces landed near Salerno, near Naples, Italy and there was a very large concentration of Allied shipping around. That was exactly the target German guided missiles and bombs were built for.

Jope's men pressed home their attacks and in the week that followed they score some hits with FRITZ X bombs causing considerable damage to the battleship **HMS WARSPITE** and the cruisers **HMS UGANDA** and **USS SAVANNAH**.

The Salerno landings marked the high point in the fortunes of KG 100. The losses the Allies suffered there taught them the utter lesson of allowing ship convoys within range of Jope's Dornier's without fighter cover. Accordingly, the next landings at Anzio in January 1944 enjoyed the USAF fighters, and so the missile carrying Dorniers suffered heavily.

The Anzio operation underlined the tenet that the effectiveness of an air launched weapon is not better than the ability of the parent aircraft to get it within launching range of the target. In fact, Japanese operations at the end of the war were similarly ineffective.

The only other greater German success was the sinking of the cruiser **HMS SPARTAN** during the Anzio operations.

CHAPTER 11

Surviving Under Duress

Sharkhunters Member Walter Kern is a veteran of the Wehrmacht and he tells about it.

We all react differently under stress, especially when imprisoned as POW's. That is a unique experience. Only those who have suffered under equal conditions can truly realize the personal predicament. All of us have our own mechanism of survival. Reactions vary from strong to weak, to just hanging on.

After World War Two a controversial issue arose around Col. Hermann Graf during his time in Soviet Prison Camps. Graf basically sympathized with the Russian cause, without actually flying or serving in their military. He was, what many simply describe, exercising his personal approach to human survival. It did not help him much since he was still kept for five years in POW camps.

Other German pilots in POW camps shunned him and even labeled him a traitor after his return to Germany. Notably Major Hans '*ASSI*' Hahn was the foremost proponent, calling Graf a coward. Hahn was already years in Soviet camps by the time Graf arrived. He expected Graf, a highly decorated, successful fighter pilot to set an example and tell the Russians where to go at every turn. Graf differed with him. Was he a coward?

WAS HE A COWARD?

Graf hailed from a simple family. His Luftwaffe fighter pilot's career was at first slow, since he was considered an old man because by 1942 he was already over 30. But once he had discovered his aiming skill, his successes came quickly. Within 13 months, he achieved 200 air victories!

In total, he flew 830 combat missions and is officially credited with 212 air victories, including ten US four-engined bombers. 202 victories were over Soviet aircraft. He personally claimed 252 aircraft, but in the strict German rule of accountability, no witness - no credit, so he had to settle for less, as did many others.

212 CONFIRMED VICTORIES

Ironically, he received no credit for his last two victories, two US P-51 Mustangs which were accompanying a bomber raid on Bremen in 1944. During the melee of the ensuing dogfight, he shot down one P-51 Mustang. In turn, he was badly shot up by the others. In a last desperate attempt, he flung his crippled Me 109 into the path of the lead Mustang, cutting it in half. Severely wounded, he spent months in a military hospital and never flew again. No one can accuse Graf of being a coward in combat.

Graf, the first to achieve 200 air victories, was awarded the ***DIAMONDS*** as the fifth German soldier on 16 September 1942. His last assignment was as Kommodore of Jagdgeschwader 52 where Major Erich Hartmann was Commanding Officer of the First Group.

Per Erich Hartmann, the German Luftwaffe High Command had anticipated the Russian desire on the two and sent a wire:

> 'GRAF AND HARTMANN BOTH FLY IMMEDIATELY TO DORTMUND AND SURRENDER TO BRITISH FORCES - ALL OTHER JG-52 PERSONNEL WILL SURRENDER AT DEUTSCH BROD TO THE SOVIETS'
>
> **GENERAL SEIDEMANN**
> **AIR FLEET COMMAND**

Graf disobeyed the order and explained to Hartmann:

> *'Look out there, Bubi. Over two thousand women, children and old people - relatives of wing personnel, refugees fleeing from the Russians - all of them defenseless. Do you think that I can jump in a Me-109 and fly to Dortmund and just leave them?'*

'I agree with you. It would be wrong for us to leave. We can't do it.'

Replied Hartmann.

> *'I'm glad you agree. So we can forget the order and stay with our people. We also forget submitting to the Russians.'*

Together they surrender to the advancing US Combat Forces on May 8, 1945. The stupid orders of the US High Command turned the entire group of 3,000 naively over to the Russians on May 16, 1943. Starting with the rape of the women, a most horrified history began to take its course.

To possibly better understand and relate to the portions describing the period of Soviet incarceration of Graf, it may be helpful to consult statements of his fellow prisoners, specifically Major Erich Hartmann and Major Hartmann Grasser. Both men distanced themselves from Graf during the time of imprisonment. Hartmann simply looked at Graf as having selected a path that he could not follow - so they separated. Grasser was much harder and bitterly opposed Graf's action in submitting to the Russians.

Even Hartmann mused later whether his strong personal stand and attitude proved to be worth an extra five years, which he served longer than Graf. Hartmann did not come home until 1955 after Bundeskanzler Konrad Adenauer had journeyed to Moscow and parlayed a German understanding for the remaining prisoners kept in Soviet Stalags! By the late 1960's festering wounds began to heal and both men mellowed on the issue. In retrospect Grasser's final assessment in 1968 summed it up when he said:

> *'I was hard during my prison time in Russia. I criticized another if he left the straight line. But now I have more experience in life and a sight more tolerance. I have a better understanding for human weakness. That is why I am not hard against Hermann Graf as some others are.'*

Finally in 1970, Graf received belated post-war recognition when he presented to the Military Museum in Rastatt the rudder of his former *Me-109* from the Stalingrad time in 1942, with 202 air victories painted on it.

Graf died in 1988. Former spunky Major *'ASSI'* Hahn, with 108 air victories, had preceded him in 1982. The formidable Major Hartmann Grasser, victor in 103 air battles, followed in 1986. And the last of the group, Major and later Colonel Erich *'Bubi'* Hartmann, undisputed *ACE OF ACES* with 352 victories, joined them in 1994.

HARTMANN   Hahn   Grasser

Colonel Erich Hartmann became a Sharkhunters Member in early 1993, a little more than a year later, he received his *'Final Orders'*.

CHAPTER 12

The Gallant Gallands

Sharkhunters Member Walter Kern is a veteran of the Wehrmacht and he remembers this famous family. Here we see Walter during the 'Battle of the Bulge. Here is story about the Galland brothers.

We reported previously on the death of one of World War Two's most famous fighter aces, the indestructible Lieutenant General Adolf Galland. His accomplishments, darings and what the French label as Civil Courage will always stand out, for obvious reasons. Was it not the dashing and outspoken Adolf Galland who asked Reichsmarschall Göring for a squadron of Spitfires to better protect the bombers during the Luftwaffe's attack on Britain? And was it not he, who was the born fighter pilot but had to give up hunting to become the youngest Luftwaffe General to take command over the entire fighter wings following the ultimately and tragic death of Werner Mölders?

Were there other Gallands? And what happened to them?

There were four brothers in all. As a close family, everybody had a nickname. Fritz, the oldest was *'Toby'*. Adolf was *'Keffer'*. Wilhelm-Ferdinand was *'Wutz'*. When Paul arrived as the last child, everybody expected a girl, so he was called *'Paulinchen'* or sometimes *'Paula'*.

They all served in the Luftwaffe as officers through the connection of Adolf, especially the two youngsters had begged for their brother's help. Later, Adolf would feel some guilt for having charted his brothers' careers. They were all good pilots. Fritz served out the war as a reconnaissance and fighter pilot.

Adolf Galland was a Sharkhunters Member from 1993 until his *'Final Orders'*.

'Wutz' and Paul became true fighter pilots in JG 26, set on following the success of the big brother Adolf. They both accounted well for themselves. Whenever others inquired about their plans after the war, both always replied that they would not be around then. Their predictions indeed came true. The youngest of the family, 22 year old Paul, was developing *'Experte'* with seventeen confirmed air victories, when he was shot down and killed over the Channel Front on 13 October, 1942.

In a letter to *'Onkel Theo'* the esteemed General Osterkamp, *'Wutz'* wrote explaining his feelings upon the air death of his younger brother.

"I cannot explain to you how immensely sad the loss of 'Paula' made me. The days with my suffering parents were the most painful, which I ever experienced in my life. I could not imagine until that time what it meant to lose this brother & friend. What he meant to me in life you know, dear Theo.

Days are behind me, when the fact that I would never see the sunny PG (Paul Galland) caused me physical pain. The work and operation in the squadron, and not in the least the tact and superb comradeship of my fellow officers, did me good. I make efforts to remember 'Paula' with pride and loving memories.

When I fly over the Channel, over his grave, I always see his content, sparkling happy face, which he will keep eternally, since he fulfilled his highest duty.

I would give a fortune if I could sit at the fireplace with you and empty my heart. It now has been clearly established that PG, in the correct assessment of the situation, through his attack saved a shot-up JABO's life, who was chased by 3 Spitfires. He fell in this fight. Shortly before, he had shot down a Boston in flames. I cannot write about it anymore, later we will talk about all!!!"

The message, full of personal grief, also reflected '*Wutz's*' keen interest in the harmony of his fighter and difficulties with certain officer's attitude. He was even sensitive to the tragedy of his brother's death when a fellow officer callously called him from the local '*girl hangout*', the infamous Hotel de la Gare (the Hotel at the Railroad Station).

Not quite ten months later 'Wutz' would join his brother when he met his fighter pilot's death during the epic air battle of August 17, 1943. It was on this day that the Eighth Air Force launched the first long-range, double daylight raid on the Messerschmitt factory at Regensburg and the ball bearing plants at Schweinfurt. The Luftwaffe shot down 60 Fortresses.

Leading II/JG 26 (2nd Group; 26th Fighter Wing) against the big bombers on their way back from Schweinfurt, '*Wurtz*' shot down a B-17 in a frontal attack, bringing his total tally to 55, including eight B-17 bombers.

He was shot down and killed by P-47 Thunderbolts of the 56th Fighter Group, '*Hub*' Zemke's Wolfpack, who unexpectedly swooped in from the east, and bounced the German group during another attack run on the B-17's.

Hub Zemke photo left

Major '*Wutz*' Galland's remains were discovered two months later, buried with the wreckage of his FW 190 twelve feet deep in the soft soil near Mastrict, in Belgium.

And now that the last **Knight of the DIAMONDS**, Adolf Galland, has joined his brothers more than 50 years later, history can finally close the curtain on the famous Galland brothers. Combined, they brought down 176 enemy aircraft and served their country in the best tradition of the family named Galland.

CHAPTER 13

Flying Combat with the Luftwaffe II

Remembered by Sharkhunters Member and former Luftwaffe flier Baron Georg von Zirk. Here is his wartime CV:

Navigator/Bombardier; Pathfinder and Target Marker; 81 Combat Missions (65 were Night Ops); Service from 8 August, 1941 through 5 May, 1945. Prisoner of the Communists June 1945 through May 1947. Served with the *Afrika Korps* in Italy and in combat with *Kampfgeschwader 'GREIF'* and *KG 4 'General Wever'* (Bomber Wings) *IV Fliegerkorps, Luftflotte 6 IV Flying Corps*, 6th *Air Fleet*, Eastern Front

The recent article in our Magazine about *Tante Ju* reminded me of the war and my own experience with her.

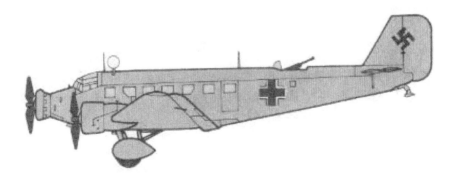

EDITOR NOTE – Tante is the German word for Aunt, and so we have Aunt Ju, a term of endearment for this plane.

The first time I saw the JU-52 was during the Polish campaign. I was still a civilian then and never thinking, that three years later, I would be flying with the Luftwaffe myself. I was quite excited when swarms of those birds were flying low over our heads. The Germans were using the JU's for transporting their wounded back to Germany. Each had red crosses painted on the fuselage. Our farm was right on the mission course of the Luftwaffe planes attacking Warsaw. So since the beginning of the war, groups of Heinkels He-111 and Stukas were flying right past us.

I remember, when on the third day of the war, a squadron of Stukas arrived over our farm and began circling overhead. They were trying out their machine guns and I could see the tracers in the sky. Suddenly two of them pulled up and dove straight down toward us, with their sirens screaming. It was a terrifying experience. Luckily for us, they didn't drop any bombs.

I saw Polish troops retreating on the nearby highway. Suddenly a HE-111 (photo below) swooped down on them and strafed them with cannons and machine guns. The next day I saw a low flying Heinkel drop bombs in the nearby forest. Trees were blasted like matchsticks, high into the air.

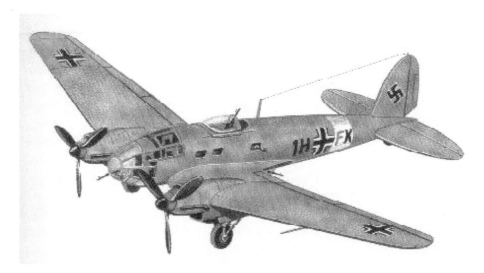

On the fifth day, German troops arrived on our farm and set up gun positions. They began shooting and the Poles were firing back with their guns. All hell broke loose. Shells were hitting all around us. One landed in our yard and set a straw stack on fire. Dad could put out the fire. The only casualty was one of our pigs. But two days later, sad news reached us. My uncle, aunt, and cousin, who had a farm nine km from us, had been murdered by Polish soldiers, because they were German. Terrible atrocities were committed to German civilians by both Polish civilians and soldiers - all over Poland. 49,000 ethnic Germans, who were Polish citizens, were killed.

EDITOR NOTE – We read of this in Chapter Two. Photo below is another of the tragic weeks prior to the invasion of Poland by the Wehrmacht.

After 27 days, the Polish army surrendered and the campaign was over. I went back to high school, but not for long. I volunteered to the Luftwaffe, and my life changed forever.

Later in 1943, when I was flying combat with KG 55 on the Southern Front in Russia, one time I had a chance to take a flight in a JU-52. Flying at low level and slow along the river Dniepr to the Black Sea was a memorable experience. I took photos, as we passed villages and waved at the people.

Reading the story by Bob Goebel (American fighter *ACE* and Sharkhunters Member), it reminded me of an experience I had during the bombing raid on Wiener Neustadt. It was in spring 1945, and I was there. Our group was posted in a village several kilometers from town.

It was heavy overcast that day, when American bombers attacked the town. We watched, as in barely two hours time, bombs destroyed the whole town.

Next day it was clear sky. In the afternoon several Mustangs swooped down on us low and attacked our Heinkels were parked in a nearby forest. Two were set on fire. One Mustang attacked a passing train, and destroyed the locomotive.

High above us we heard the drone of B-24 bombers. We saw and heard our fighters shooting at them. From one bomber we saw three men bail out, but no more, the plane kept on flying. The formation broke up and scattered. Some bombers turned east, towards Hungary, where the Russian army was approaching. The American crew came down where we were waiting, and we took them to our Squadron Headquarters. There they were interrogated. They had flown from a base in Italy.

I had a letter from my pilot, Werner Frick (Sharkhunters Member). He is very pleased with his Membership & magazines. He says, 'Vielen Dank!'

Regarding this, he writes, Wilhelm Johnen (Sharkhunters Member) was a former comrade of his. They were together in Advanced Pilot School at Alt-Loennewitz and later in *Zerostörerschule* (ME-110) at München-Schleissheim, in 1940/41. Afterwards Johnen became a Nightfighter and earned the Ritterkreuz. Frick was transferred to Regensburg for testing the *Lastensegler* (Gigant). He towed it in a '*Trojka Schlepp*' which means with three ME-110s and later three Heinkels.

Lastensegler – it means 'Burdens Sailer'

My ex wife was also in the Luftwaffe. She served as Luftwaffen-Helferin at Göring's headquarters at Potsdam. She had joined the Luftwaffe in 1943 at the age of 17 and served until the end of war.

As a teletypist, she handled important orders from and to the front, going through there. She saw Göring on many occasions. She saw also first-hand, how the war was sabotaged on our side, by delaying, falsifying orders, sending supplies to the wrong destinations, etc. She was in charge of over sixty LH girls. Their Headquarters was bombed many times, and she saw 60 girls die in raids. She got to the point that she didn't care to go to the bomb shelter any more. At the end of the war, her outfit was evacuated to Denmark. There they surrendered to the British army.

CHAPTER 14

The Disastrous Kassel Mission

From Sharkhunters Member and Wehrmacht Veteran Walter Kern

On September 27, 1996 I attended a unique gathering of World War Two fliers - the 52nd anniversary of the Kassel Mission. Nearly 300 participants, relatives and guests were present. But most remarkably, the leadership of the *'Kassel Mission Memorial Society'* had invited their former foes, the German fighter pilots and their families, to attend the gathering.

As a guest during the three-day meeting, I was privileged to witness the camaraderie among the *'old and seasoned'* fliers and their courtesy toward their German guests. It brought forth the best in people who could, after half a century, look more objectively at the time of that epic of the Eagles in the air over Europe.

What is this *'Kassel Mission Memorial Society'* all about? It is the result of an intense idea by William R. Dewey, a former pilot and participant of the Kassel Mission. He wanted to reunite all participants in a common bond society, and to pay tribute to those who sacrificed their lives. It all dates back to a day in 1944 - Wednesday, September 27 to be exact - when the Eighth Air Force in England launched an all-out bombing effort on Germany. A total of 1,092 four-engined B-17 Flying Fortresses and B-24 Liberators were dispatched to various targets over the Reich. Accompanied by 678 fighters, it was a well protected air armada, destined for an early morning attack.

The 445th Bomb Group, comprised of the 700th Bomb Squadron leading the 701, 702 and 703 Bomb Squadrons with thirty-nine B-24 Liberators was part of a strike force of two hundred eighty three bombers scheduled to bomb Kassel, site of the Henschel Works, manufacturers of the formidable Tiger tanks. Four aircraft aborted, sending the remaining thirty-five aircraft to the aircraft. This entire formation was protected by thirty-five P-47 Thunderbolts, twenty-five P-38 Lighnings and one hundred fifty eight P-51 Mustange.

The solid overcast prevented a visual bombing requiring target sighting via radar. Shortly before reaching Kassel, the 445th Group lead plane piloted by Captain John Chilton with Flight Commander Major Donald McCoy (C.O. of 700th Squadron) in charge of the group, shifted course away from the main bomber stream and headed toward Göttingen some twenty-five miles to the northeast of Kassel. When his fellow aircraft pilots noted the deviation and radioed back to Chilton, they were advised to keep it tight, follow the lead and maintain silence.

The reason for this course change has never been fully explained. Some quote a navigational error by the lead navigator, others blame a faulty instrument. In view of the strong visibility of the other aircraft it almost appears that the official Eighth Air Force written Mission Report for that date indicates that thirty-five aircraft were to bomb Göttingen is correct.

Of course this report was generated after the mission and this data could have been conveniently inserted to bear out the facts. As it stands today, it remains a mystery. You will see why nobody wants to take responsibility for the course change.

The 445th with its four Bomb Squadrons heading away from the protection of the fighters aimed for Göttingen. The tight flight formation of the thirty-five B-24 Liberators presented the following Box Pattern:
- 700 Bomb Squadron with ten aircraft in the lead;
- 702 Bomb Squadron with ten aircraft high right;
- 701 Bomb Squadron with seven aircraft high, high right;
- 703 Bomb Squadron with eight aircraft low left

At 0942, on command of the lead aircraft via the release of a smoke bomb, the formation dropped one hundred eighty five 1,000 pound GP bombs from an altitude of 23,000 feet through the solid overcast. The official Eighth Air Force Bombing Evaluation Report noticed:

RESULTS UNKNOWN

As it was, all bombs fell harmlessly in the open fields between three small villages a short distance before Göttingen. The only damage reported by the Germans related to a few farm buildings, a garden plot and an ox who was injured and had to be slaughtered.

After dropping their bomb load, the 445th executed a southern and then westerly course, some distance behind the main force that attacked Kassel then headed for home. German fighters, alerted to the oncoming armada, had taken off from nearby fields to intercept the Kassel force. Guided by their radar control, they inserted themselves between the main US bomber stream and the straying 445th. Whether the German control was aware that the 445th had no fighter cover is not known. Three German assault groups (Sturmgruppen) of the Luftwaffe's Reichs Defense attacked in consecutive waves. These were:
- II/JG 4
- IV/JG 3
- II/JG 300

The German tactic called for a heavily protected 'Storm Fighter' to break through the strongly defended attacking Allied formation of robust and heavily armed B-17 and B-24 bombers with no consideration of the hail of fire, with the aim of destroying the bomber unit. The appropriate fighter for this task was a converted Fw 190 A8/R2.

The reliable and sturdy BMW Type 801, 14 cylinder radial engine powered this overloaded monster, which, with an additional fuel tank, held almost 260 gallons to provide a three hour flight time, reached a weight of seven to eight tons. It was clearly inferior in dogfights with enemy fighters, but it was very well protected against the .50 cal. machine gun fire from the bombers.

Equipped with armored oil cooler, bullet-proof windshield, 6mm fireproof plates on the cabin sides, 9mm armor plate behind the pilot's seat, the aircraft was designed as a formidable flying gun platform. Firepower was awesome! Two heavy .50 cal. machine guns for long range, two 20mm automatic cannons above the cowlings and two 30mm wing guns for range closer than 600 yards. The latter was called the *'jackhammer'* because of its staccato noise. It only took two or three rounds of this highly explosive to blow up a heavy bomber.

These heavily armored Fw 190's called 'Rqmmbock' had to be escorted by more nimble Me 109's for protection from swift US fighters. The combined force of about ninety German aircraft fell upon the 445th. The first attack with aircraft aligned in a long line abreast coming from the rear, was flown by II/JG4 (Second Group Fighter Wing 4) led by Wing Commander Michalski followed by the second wave of IV/JG3 and Captain Moritz while Lt. Bretschneider came last with his II/JG3.

The entire attack lasted only several minutes starting at 1103 hours. The Fw 190 'Sturmböcke' or 'Rammböcke (Storm Fighters or Ramming Fighters) passed through the bomber formation from astern with their 20mm firing and, at close range of less then 600 yards, the awesome 30mm cannons blazing. The sky was full of bright flashes from exploding shells.

Frank Bertram, 445th BombGru, 702 BombRon, lead navigator reported:
'Someone called off a dogfight to the rear of the group. Then someone else said - here comes our fighter protection. At this moment I looked out the side window and saw little puffs of black, the size of basketballs. My instant reaction was - What kind of FLAK is this? It is so small and so unbelievably accurate at our level - the Jerry ground gunners are amazing! I did not put two and two together until I saw out 'radial engine fighter protection' come up and peel off. Those P-47's I had imagined turned into Fw 190's with all guns going full blast.'

Leo Pouiliot, co-pilot, 445th Group, 703 Bomb Squadron recalls:

'......for some reason, things did not go as it was briefed to us. The bomb run was much too long. Finally - the smoke bombs from the lead plane were dropped. We made a turn to the right and resumed our course out. Again I remarked how good the formation looked.

After about ten minutes, things started to happen. The tail gunner of Cecil Isom's ship (to our right) started to fire at something. Then I noticed small white puffs appearing throughout our formation, and realized that we were jumped by enemy fighters. I was on the Fighter Channel and started to call for some escort. I called BALANC 3-1, 3-2 and 3-3 and was answered immediately. I told them we were having trouble. They inquired about our position and I switched the jackbox to the intercom to get our position from Milton Fandler, the navigator. Then our plane got several hits in the waist and the radio was knocked out. Looking to the right, I saw just plain hell. Planes were going down, some in flames, others just exploding. The air was full of 20mm shells. I thought the whole German Air Force was in the air at the same time. The first pass that they made took most of the squadron with them. In the 703rd only Isom's and our ship was left. There was no one to protect us from the rear. Enemy fighters were all over the sky. Our plane was shaking like a leaf in a good blizzard from the guns, all firing at the same time. On the right, a B-24 with its number three engine tank on fire, blew up and three of the men got out the waist. The air was full of debris of burning planes and chutes. Some of the boys pulled their chute too soon and the silk caught on fire. They went plummeting to the earth.'

Werner Vorberg, Luftwaffe Squadron Captain II Sturm/JG4 whose group flew on that day, its first Sturm mission against the US Air Force; the 445th Bomb Group. He recalls:

'After taking off from Welzow (south of Berlin) under the protection of two groups of Me 109 escort fighters and after repeated course changes and coming undisturbed by enemy fighters, the unit reached the Liberators and flew from behind into the stream of bombers that were numerically superior to us. We divided up and flew against the individual ships. Whoever was not shot down by the bombers had success or had to ram.

After passage from the back of the formation to the front, shot down ships were observed. Crews from four-engined planes flying further ahead were bailing out in rows before they were even attacked. Ten or twelve bombers exploded in the air, although they had already dropped their bombs. That also led to collision when opening fire. After the march through the entire stream of bombers, we distanced ourselves quickly by swinging down from the place where the battle took place in order not to be caught by enemy fighters. On my return to Welzow, a wheel along with its shot up support fell off when I let down my landing gear. I had to land on my belly. Our losses included ten machines, one Squadron Captain and six other pilots. Three pilots were wounded and one rammed his target.'

The pilot who rammed his B-24 target was Heinz Pappenberg, living today in Germany, flew his first mission as a *'Sturm'* or Assault Fighter. Coming from the *Polar Fighter Group*, he had volunteered for the *'Sturmgruppen'* assignment. He reported that his weapons failed, so he rammed the tail unit of a B-24, bringing the aircraft down. In doing so, he severely injured both knees and was unable to fly until the end of the war.

The German Luftwaffe Fighter Division Ground Controller had successfully all three fighter groups (*Sturmgruppen*) around the vastly superior numbered Allied fighter aircraft protection. The Kassel contingent of the US bomber attack force consisting of three hundred fifteen bombers alone had an escort of over two hundred fighters of which one hundred fifty eight were Mustangs.

Through skillful vectoring, the adept Luftwaffe Ground Control simultaneously consolidated the *"Sturmgruppen"* to arrive within minutes of each other, just behind the unescorted 445th Bomb Group. In the precious few minutes that followed the first sighting, every German fighter aircraft of the three *"Sturmgruppen"* successfully attacked from the rear, storming through the entire flight information of four squadrons of the 445th Bomber Group consisting of thirty-five aircraft. Operating at the usual formation speed for B-24's at about 165mph, the much faster German fighters raced through four staggered squadrons at better than 350-370 mph. That is a speed advantage of about 200 mph or close to 300 feet per second. The fighters started firing at about 600 yards and it took about six seconds to point blank range. A bomber needed only two hits by the devastating 30mm shells to doom it.

Flying through the estimated 2,000 yards long formation required about another 20-25 seconds, so that each German fighter was exposed to defensive fire for about half a minute. All three German fighter waves, the II Sturm of JG 300, the IV Sturm of JG 3 (Udet) and the II Sturm of JG 4 attacking in sequence, timed almost to perfection, ripped through the B-24 squadrons at about a one minute interval. So, the entire battle did not consume more than five or six minutes.

Ernst Schroeder, a young Luftwaffe fighter pilot in the II Sturm/JG 300 recalls that fateful day:

"At 10am our group took off from Finsterwalde in our FW-190's for an enemy engagement against a bomber formation consisting perhaps of thirty aircraft. We climbed through a layer of clouds to reach our attack altitude of 7,500-8,000 meters (25,000 to 26,000 feet) where the US formation was reported. We were led to the bombers by our Y-Command of the fighter division. Because we were flying above the clouds we could not see the ground. With the constantly changing course following the orders we actually had no idea where we were. We did not use our radios being busy flying the ever changing course and just followed the ground radar guided direction. Around 11 AM, after flying in a variety of patterns but steadily to the west, the ground commander became more and more agitated, telling us we should visually pick up the enemy aircraft right in front of us. Indeed we did.

The aircraft of this bomber formation consisting of B-24 Liberators flew right ahead of us at a similar altitude. It was like a swarm of mosquitoes, but soon the silhouettes became bigger and bigger because of our great speed. Suddenly several of these big ships began to burn and plunge down with fire and smoke - even before we had fired a single shot. A fighter unit flying ahead of us had begun the attack. Immediately the sky became full of parachutes and wreckage, and we were flying straight into it.

My squadron commander and I had installed a new aiming device. This unit included a series of very rapidly running gyros that automatically calculated the necessary aiming allowance. Because of this, we could fire rather precisely and effectively from a greater distance than normal. The results were impressive for me.

Before I had closed in on my selected target to the normal firing range, my bomber stood already in flames as a result of my six guns. Both engines on the left were fiercely burning. The aircraft turned on its side and plunged earthward. The neighboring ship was already smoking from a previous attack. I only needed to change my aim slightly to fire again. The new aiming device was working astonishingly. I was so surprised and fascinated that I flew alongside my victim as the meter-high flames poured out of the Liberator, well beyond its twin rudder. Then this great machine clumsily laid itself on its back and went down. All of this happened much faster than you can read it here.

In view of this surprising success, I naturally wanted to know where my to opponents would fall. This was necessary because a double shootdown of two four-engined bombers (they were also my only ones) was for us in 1944, something exceptional. Therefore I circled the crashing wreckage of my two adversaries in large downward running spirals. But my intention was hindered in a most horrible way, because the entire sky was filled with fliers in parachutes who had jumped, and small and large chunks of airplane debris which suddenly appeared in front of my high diving speed of 600-700 km/st (375-435 mph). I truly had to close my eyes often because I believed I would run into something.

Under me came the cloud layer through which here and there the surface of the earth was quickly shimmering - closer and closer. Through this cloud cover rose ten to fifteen columns of smoke from the explosions of the crashing aircraft. I flew through the relative thin cloud layer, which now spread itself at an altitude of about 1,000 meters above the ground.

Below me lay a valley of forest covered mountainsides. Through the valley ran a stretch of double railroad tracks and on it stood a long train. The smoke of the locomotive climbed vertically. This image has clearly imprinted itself on me until today. When I close my eyes, I see it clearly before me.

Where had the two bombers fallen? Everywhere was burning wreckage. The fields were covered with white parachutes, where American and certainly also German fliers had come down.

I arrived at almost 100 meters above the ground and could clearly see crewmen, who had bailed out, running through the fields. When I flew over them, they stood still and clearly raised their hands high. Also I saw people already - perhaps also soldiers and policemen - running toward them to take them captive. My intention to recognize the locality through some distinguishing landmark failed completely.

Something suddenly happened which quickly broke me away from my intention. I was, as stated, only about 100 meters above the ground, when diagonally from the front an airplane with a yellow nose shot towards me - an American fighter unmistakable of the P-51B type. In the wink of an eye we had raced closely by each other on an opposite course and hurried both of our machines again on an opposite course, so that we flew towards one another like jousting knights of the Middle Ages.

Both of us opened simultaneous with our big caliber weapons. The American immediately made a hit on my tail section. My weapons, on the other hand, failed after a few shots. When we had flown by once another, the maneuver began anew. Since I could not fire a shot, I began to fly with evasive movements the moment the American opened fire, so that he could no longer aim correctly. It was a strange feeling each time looking into the flash of his six 50 .cal guns. After we had played this little game for five or six times, there was only the possibility to fly low over the ground immediately after his flight over me and to rush off immediately. I was successful. After his turn, in which he always pulled up sharply, the camouflage paint on the top of my plane made it difficult for the American to find my plane against the dappled ground.

I landed after minutes of fearful sweating at 11:30 am at the Langensala Airport after a total of 90 minutes of flight time. On inspection of my machine showed some hits in the tail section. A part of the covering of my rudder was torn off. The damage was so slight that I could take off again at noon. I landed at 12:15pm at Erfurt-Bindersleben, where my bird had to be repaired in the hanger.

My aircraft was the heavily armored FW-190-A8-R2 which, due to its weight was inferior to the American fighter planes in aerial combat. This Focke-Wulf was superior to bombers who had minimal armor protection. The rugged double star air-cooled BMW engine developed 1,800 HP and was quite able to take punishment from the .50cal machine guns of the bombers. I had on board four MG/151 20 mm guns plus two 13mm (50 cal) heavy machine guns. Some aircraft had even two 30mm cannons. The explosive power of our ammunition against a poorly armored bomber was absolutely devastating.

My aircraft was marked as "RED 19" with the slogan "Kölle Alaaf" meaning "Cologne Aloft" because I was born in Cologne."

Theodore J. Myers, flying as engineer and top turret gunner with the 703 Bomb Squadron, 445th Bomb Group, recollects:

We were on our way home after having bombed Kassel (actually off Göttingen) flying at approx 10:15 AM, somewhere in Central in Germany.

I flew in the top turret. I was the first one on our crew to see them and to report them to the crew. They were lined up, wing tip to wing tip, and were coming in low at 5 o'clock (I guess this was because we had no lower ball turrets in any of our planes).

We were one of the first ships of the group to go down in flames. I saw several chutes in the air while I was firing. I fired my guns until they became so hot that they kept jamming until finally couldn't charge them anymore. A shell exploded near the top of my turret and it looked like one of my guns was bent. The smoke of that shell got on the glass and I couldn't see out. I pressed the interphone switch to call the pilot and found that it wasn't working.

When my feet touched the flight deck I felt a heavy vibration. I looked forward and saw the pilot and the co-pilot. The radio operator was sitting on the floor with his flak suit and helmet on. They all seemed all right at that time.

I looked into the bomb bay and saw several large streams of gasoline shooting down against the bomb bay doors. A mist of gasoline was floating forward onto the flight deck. The first thing was entered my mind was to try to stop the gas flow. If those shells ever entered the ship, with all that gasoline squirting around, that ship would explode. So I climbed down into the bomb bay to look at the holes in the gasoline tanks, hoping they would seal themselves. The holes were too large to seal up, so I decided to open the bomb bay doors to let the slipstream blow it out of the ship. During that time I got soaked from head to foot with gasoline. The slipstream started to clear the inside. I turned around to get on the flight deck (all of this took less than a minute) to tell the pilot we had been hit bad and were losing gas fast. Before I could move, one or more 20mm shells went off under my feet, wounding me in the right foot and both legs. The blow lifted me up and hurt back and I fell on my back on the catwalk. Then I saw a blinding flash and I was on fire from head to foot. I felt my face burning and that was all I remembered was I thought I was dying.

I guess I had lost consciousness. In a minute or two I awoke and found myself hanging in my parachute. The slipstream had blown out the fire. My face was so burned that I could only see out of my left eye. I saw a big streaming mass of fire go by me about 200 or 300 feet away. I am sure the ship exploded about that time.

I met the tail gunner Frank T. Plesa, who was badly wounded and burned, five or six hours later in a German hospital. He said he had been blown out of his turret. He saw the wing of his ship go past him. Then he lost consciousness and came to about 800 feet above the ground and pulled the rip cord. Plesa said that just before the ship caught fire he saw the left waist gunner Everette L. Williams, a fellow flying his last mission, get badly wounded.'

Oberleutnant Oskar Romm, Squadron Leader IV Sturm/JG 3 (Udet), seasoned veteran of JG 52 from the Eastern Front, holder of the **KNIGHTS CROSS** with 92 aerial victories during his career recalls this of the Kassel Mission:

Our combat formation was led towards the enemy formation by the ground radio stations. After visual contact was established in the air, the leader of the combat formation was given clearance to attack.

As the Squadron Leader of the 15th Squadron, I had a good tactical position within the combat formation and attacked a flight of three bombers.

Just like during the downing of a four-engine bomber over Oschersleben on July 7, 1944, my approach for the attack was divided into three actions, going off real quick. First to fire into the fuselage to hit the machine gun positions, then hit the pilot's compartment, and finally to hit and set fire to two engines and one side of the aircraft. If two engines on one side were on fire, aeronautical control over the plane was almost immediately put out of action.

I first attacked (in the manner above) the bomber on the left position of the flight, then the one on the right and lastly the leading B-24 of the flight. I then pulled up in a steep turn and, while flying over them, observed them going down spinning, burning, and breaking off of wings in the area of the burning engines.

The film from my gun cameras showed the downing, demonstrating in an appalling way the location of the hits and the effects of the shots on the three aircraft. The most devastating damage was done by the two MK 108 30mm guns.

I opened up the aerial combat by first firing the two 13mm (50 cal) machine guns, then the two 30mm guns, and between less than 400 meters (about 1,300 feet) and ramming distance, with all six guns firing off short bursts.

On the next day, September 28, 1944, I again took off against penetrating US bombers in their mission to Kassel. I downed, in the usual manner, two Boeing B-17 Fortress bombers. Subsequent aerial combat with Lockheed P-38 Lightning fighters was without results.'

It had all started so innocently and total routine, reports Paul M. Dickerson, crew member of a B-24 - 703rd Bomb Squadron, 445th Bomb Group:

'The 27th of September 1944 started out as a typical day in the ETO. We members of the Cecil J. Isom crew (703rd Bomb Squadron) were awakened at the awful time of 02:30 hrs. One hour later we were briefed on the mission and then got our breakfast, followed by the tedious checking of all our weapons and the functions of the aircraft. We were off the ground at 07:15.

Together with the other aircraft we circled until we got into formation and proceeded to the target. Our navigator, Art Shay, advised that we were not on course, but we were Squadron Lead and not Group Lead. The Base Navigator, a Major, was flying with the Group Lead crew and he was in charge of navigation.

In waves of ten and fifteen FW-190's poured in on us. Machine guns were firing.....everywhere B-24's, Me-190's and FW-190's were falling. Some were blazing, some were smoking and some were blown to bits. The air was full of parachutes, pandemonium reigned! A German with a black parachute drifted by our right window. Bill Wagner took a bead on him, then looked at me. I said "no", and Wagner let him drift by. I could see the pilot plainly. He was close. One burst and I'd have had him. Ray Phillips, our tail gunner, got one FW-190, as did Shay, riding in the nose turret, and Wagner. Kyle Baily, top turret gunner got two FW-190's.

Then all was quiet. We waited for the kill. We knew we could not last longer. We were dead men and we knew it. By now there remained only about seven of the original formation of thirty five. Three of the seven were too crippled to fight back. We were hopeless and helpless.

But the Germans did not come back. There wasn't much left of them either. Then we saw the most beautiful sight & we knew why the Germans left. The sight of our fighters was unmistakable.

At 10:00 hrs. we were a squadron of ten B-24's.
At 10:06 hr. were a squadron of two!

When we returned to our base we found the plane in front of us firing red flares for emergency landing. There were injured on board. The tower wanted to knew where the rest of the group was. They wanted to know why we were alone and asking for landing instructions. We told them, that **WE WERE THE GROUP**!

By the time we landed and were getting our gear from the plane, we were surrounded by M.P.'s. ***We were told not to talk to anyone.*** They whisked us off to a debriefing room and locked us up. We were asked question after question, as if they were trying to catch us in some kind of lie.

Colonel Jimmy Stewart (the famous movie star, who at the time was the Executive Officer of the 703rd Bomb Squadron) arrived from Wing Headquarters and took charge of the meeting. Since he was a veteran of many combat missions and had led us on missions, he was aware of what could happen and seemed to understand as he calmed the meeting and listening intently.

Only a Handful Left Alive

It was time for the evening meal when we were told we could leave the debriefing room. When we went to the chow hall, where food had been prepared for several hundred, there were only about two dozen of us that went to eat. Again there was disbelief when we told them that we were all that was left. Our meal was a quiet solemn one in that big empty chow hall. No one was talking.

Things were quiet in our almost empty hut. God only knows why we were there. The next day we sat quietly and watched them inventory and remove the belongings of those who did not return. We were more stunned than before, as we realized that they were really gone; that they would not be back.

On the 28th, the 445th put up ten planes on a return trip to Kassel. Our plane, the "***PATTY GIRL***", was the only plane from the previous day's mission to Kassel that was airborne for this mission. We did not fly it.
Yes......War is hell!"

When one considers the results of the bombing, the thought of the much publicized and lauded "***Precision Bombing***" technique with the Norden bombsight and radar sighting, takes a real back seat. Thirty-five aircraft with 350 skilled, brave airmen flew a scheduled mission estimated to last 7 hours 45 minutes. All of the one hundred eighty five thousand pound bombs - a total of 92.5 tons - fell way off the target. If, in fact, it was the city of Göttingen that was the aiming point, the target was failed by miles. All bombs fell harmlessly in the open fields between the villages of Rosdorf, Gross-Ellershausen and Grone without casualties or damages.

The main Kassel bomber attack force too, with the remaining two hundred forty eight bombers, achieved very poor results. Although the official Bombing Results Report lists 204.5 tons dropped on target with "Fair to Good Results", this must be considered was at best a "Sight unseen" report. Many US Army Air Corps experts must have wondered how anyone could tell with the solid overcast over the entire area.

So, not even the most optimistic bomb results evaluators nor the command staff in England had any confidence in this assessment and immediately ordered another strike for the same target the following day. The 445th Bomb Group put up ten planes for this mission. The only plane from the previous mission, which was in good enough shape to fly in this ten aircraft formation the next day back to Kassel, led by Captain Rowe Bowen was *"PATTY GIRL"*, SN 42-50811E. It flew with a different crew.

As coincidence would have it, this time, on Sept. 28, at 13:31 hrs, at different bomber squadron tried another aerial plowing of the fields around the Kassel area. Returning from a partial mission to Magdeburg, some 60 miles North-East of Kassel, B-17's Flying Fortresses of the 324th Bomb Squadron, 91st Bomb Group, First Division, led by First Lt O'Brian (A/C # 43-37844), dropped one hundred 500 pound bombs between the village of Friedlos and Bad Hersfeld. Intended target, per reports, was the Eschwege airfield, some 22 miles NE of the drop site.

The aerial engagement of the day is reflected in both the US & Luftwaffe official reports.

US Army Air Corps reports for the day total sixty-four German aircraft destroyed, with bombers claiming twenty-three enemy aircraft destroyed while the escorting fighters claimed thirty-six destroyed in the air and another five destroyed on the ground. The total claims for the day are seventy-five German aircraft including nine damaged. The US reports do not count or credit any claims by the downed bombers of the 445th.

The Luftwaffe Logs do no specifically count the losses on the 445th Bomb Group alone, but are for the entire day, reflecting the following:
Twenty-nine fighter aircraft lost including Me-109's and 25 Fw-190's. Most of the FW-190's were the heavily armored R2 types. Some were shot down by the 445th bombers while others caught by the alerted P-51 escort. The overstatement by the US Forces is standard, as many bombers often fire on the same fighter and claim it when it goes down.

Also, when German pilots firewall the throttle, and black smoke from the overcharged engine trails the aircraft and many a gunner on the US bombers mistook this for a hit and a definite victory, while in fact the German fighter was merely diving away at maximum acceleration.

US Bomber Losses of the *445th Bomb Group*:
- Aircraft scheduled for mission 40
- Aircraft available for take-off 39
- Aircraft aborted   4

Three aborted from 701 B.S. which flew the High Right position all three aircraft had assigned slots at right rear position-the most vulnerable place to be shot down by German fighters.

One aborted from 703 B.S. also from right rear position; Schneider, who ran off perimeter track and cut a tire

Aircraft attacking target   35
Shot down and crashed:
- In Germany   25
- In Belgium   1
- In France   2
- In England   1

In addition,
- Two were shot up and landed at Manston, England;
- Only four made it back to their home base at Tibenham

Only one aircraft, the *"**PATTY GIRL**"* SN 42-50811E, was in good enough shape to fly in the ten plane mission back to Kassel the next day, led by Captain Rowe Bowen.

The Available reports of the other bomber losses for this day by different bomb groups and squadrons are inconclusive because:
 Task Force 1 lists four hundred forty nine aircraft dispatched with four hundred eleven attacking, losing thirty-eight aircraft in the account.
 Task Force 2 lists four hundred fifteen aircraft dispatched with three hundred eighty four attacking, losing thirty-one aircraft in the account.
 Task Force 3 lists three hundred twenty five aircraft dispatched with two hundred eighty three attacking, losing thirty-two aircraft in the count.

Other losses summaries include two bombers shot down by AA.

One German FW-190 rammed a B-24, bringing both aircraft down and severely wounding the German pilot. Another FW-190 rammed a P-51 causing both to crash, killing each pilot.

The tragic human sacrifice by the 445th Bomb Group for the day:
- 116 killed in action, including airmen shot by Germans on the ground; and 134 taken prisoner.

On the German side reports indicate:
Eighteen pilots lost their lives, including two who were shot by US fighter planes in the air while coming down on their chutes.

With a complete results evaluation of the entire days attack on September 27, 1944, when the US Army Air Corps launched a maximum effort attack with twenty-six combat wings and fifteen escort groups on eleven key targets in the Reich, dispatching one thousand, one hundred seventy nine four-engined bombers, escorted by six hundred seventy eight fighters.

CHAPTER 15

The WALRUS

What the Hell is THAT?
By Sharkhunters Member Frank O'Shaugnasy

WARNING – Strap yourself into your favorite chair before you begin this chapter. It is hilarious and we don't want you to fall out and get hurt.

Among quotes about aircraft with which people are probably familiar are: "*An aircraft is a collection of spare parts flying in close formation*"

And "*Any landing is good, as long as you can walk away from it.*"

HMS SHROPSHIRE

Whilst the first quote is probably correct, the latter may not always be as good as it seems. During World War Two, I was on the British cruiser **HMS SHROPSHIRE**, which carried a catapult-launched reconnaissance aircraft, an amphibian, and most of our landings were made on the sea longside the ship, then we were hoisted inboard by crane. As the last person I had heard about who possibly would have walked away from this type of landing had been crucified several years before, the latter maximum did not have must relevance for me.

A word about the (forgive the slander) aeroplane - - it was a Supermarine Walrus. Most British naval aircraft had names associated with the sea. Shark, Swordfish, Barracuda among the fishes. Skua, Roc, Albacore among the feathered creatures. The Walrus being an enigma, being neither fish nor fowl. The Supermarine Company also designed another aircraft which gained some recognition during WW II called a Spitfire. The Walrus was designed, I presume, during the carefree days of the company. It was an amphibian; a flying boat; its wheels removed whilst operating from the ship to reduce weight.

I believe that some half-crazed minion at the Admiralty had seen the word '*BOAT*' in the aircraft's description and decided that it should be equipped with as many accouterments of a ship as was possible. To that end - we had an anchor, rope, bollards, boat hook and a bell - albeit a small one - to be rung only if we had the misfortune to be anchored in a sea lane in a fog! Hand-held, air-operated horns weren't invented at the time.

Last but not least, we had a heaving line - but without the lead weights and markings for taking sounding. I was informed, as I recall, that they had been removed from all similar aircraft after the pilot of a Walrus whose altimeter had quit whilst flying over London in a fog; had persuaded his observed to attempt to find their altitude. The heaving line got tangled 'round Nelson's Column. The lead weight knocked out Nelson's other eye and scared the hell out of the pigeons.

There was so much extraneous gear stored forward, i.e. in the sharp end (or bow) of the Walrus, that she seemed to assume a nose down attitude in flight. This, coupled with the somewhat less than startling speed, pusher-type engine, and high bi-plane gave her a flight pattern somewhat like a ruptured duck. This was even more emphasized if you had the misfortune to see one of these creatures after having landed on say, the Firth of Tay at Broughty Ferry, put down its wheels, and then waddle up the boat ramp to roost ashore overnight.

The aircraft was *'powered'* by a 770 hp Pegasus rotary engine; the British Navy was also keen on Greek mythology - - had a speed of about 90 knots with no headwind; and a range of about 350 miles. We always did our searches ahead of the convoy not just for strategic reasons, but for selfish ones too. Ahead, if we had trouble, you could be reasonably certain that the convoy would catch up with us. Astern, there was always the nagging thought that perhaps we couldn't catch up with them. One *'olde air gunner'* told me of Walrus being overtaken by the sailing vessel **CUTTY SARK** in the English Channel. I have always believed this should be taken with a grain of salt, but I clearly remembered a seagull screeching "**Sunday driver**!" at us as he glided by, on the inside lane one day when we returned to Freetown.

The Walrus was in all probability, the oldest airplane still on active service at the end of World War II. Affectionately known as the **'Pusser's Duck'** originally put in service in 1931, she was 14 years old at the war's end. After the war, some of them must have been used on whaling ships as I remember seeing an advertisement requesting former crewmen to apply for jobs in that line of work.

During her formative years she probably saw more of the world than any other more famous flying machine. It was used extensively in the Indian and Pacific Oceans when air routes were being surveyed between the *'far-flung outposts of the Empire'*. One of the more memorable of her exploits was that she was the first aircraft seen by descendants of the **HMS BOUNTY** mutineers living on Pitcairn Island. They apparently were not tremendously impressed. They cheered when they saw it launched by catapult from the cruiser, but appeared disgusted when it landed in the sea and was hoisted aboard by crane. Any bird could take off and land on a ship without use of mechanical devices; the Walrus obviously was not in the same class.

The crew included the '***MUSHROOM***' or Air Gunner

The aircraft carried a three-man crew consisting of Pilot, Observer and Telegraphist Air Gunner (the Navy had Telegraphists, everyone else had radio operators). The armament consisted of two Lewis guns, one aft manned by the Air Gunner and the one forward by the Observer - that is, if he could get it extracted from the mass of gear in the aforementioned shipwright's store! The guns were fed with pans of ammunition, and to this day I cannot remember whether the guns had 97 stoppages and the pans had 20 rounds; or if the reverse was true. If the reader has not had any experience with a Lewis machine gun, just ignore the last sentence. Actually, more havoc could have been created with two crossbows!

The rear gun had to be traversed and fired very carefully as in almost every direction except vertically there were bits and pieces of your own aircraft, and the other two crew members took a dim view if you shot off your own tail or riddled the wings. This of course, was a minor matter with regard to using the rear gun position - the real trouble was the fan! The engine was stated, was the pusher type and of course, the propeller was pointed backwards and where it was pointed backwards felt about three feet from your neck when you manned '*Repel boarders*' station.

You had two postures that could be assumed for the rear gun position. You could kneel down, which would result in being somewhat protected from the gale created by the '*fan*'. The hatch, when opened, had a portion which swung up at about 45 degrees and if you crouched down, you had some protection from the hurricane force winds but it was tough on the knees, and you could see even less.

If you stood, you immediately felt that roughly 70% of your body was now virtually free of the aircraft. You had the impression that the coaming of the hatch was around your ankles. You were subjected to the total effect of the propeller blast, your goggles were too loose and the wind was causing them to flap and threaten to beat your skull to a pulp.

Your eyes watered so you couldn't see and tightening the goggle straps just cut off the blood supply to your brain. You could, I suppose, have taken them off, squinted your eyes and found that your opponent had fired all his ammunition astern of you under the mistaken impression that you were heading in that direction - or, having developed his own troubles by laughing so hard that his eyes were also watering and he couldn't see either! In any event, as the majority of our flying was at sea, the only hostilities we met were seabirds.

How to get airborne - or *The WALRUS Follies!*

When the ship was at sea, the aircraft was launched by means of a catapult. At the end of its (**Ha-Ha**) mission, it landed in the sea and was hoisted aboard. In harbour there was a different method for the launch. We were hoisted overboard and dropped in the water. I will cover the simplicity of this at a later time. The aircraft on the ship was stored on the launching trolley on the catapult. The catapult was mounted behind the funnels, about 24 feet above the upper deck. It was normally ranged fore and aft and in a retracted position. To launch, the crew boarded the aircraft, the engine was started up, the catapult was rotated until it was running athwartships, the two extensions were run to, the trolley holding the aircraft was run back to the end of the catapult, the engine was revved and the crew crossed their fingers - and away we went into the wild blue yonder. Simple really, if it hadn't been for the spectators and the foreplay.

First of all, everything in the Navy is done according to a recognized drill and this provides the preliminaries (like an orchestra tuning up) for the spectators at this event. The bulge blows - it sounds like the preparation for a cavalry charge! The boatswain blows his whistle and over the Tannoy comes the clarion call:

"PREPARE TO LAUNCH AIRCRAFT!"

"AIRCRAFT HANDLING CREW TO THEIR STATIONS."

"SEA BOATS CREW AND LOWERERS OF THE DUTY WATCH TO THEIR STATIONS."

Needless to say, this call engendered a certain amount of disquiet in at least one member of the flying crew! What we were going to do; just flop off the end of the catapult. It certainly didn't help to hear the Duty Officer asking the Captain if he was sure that he knew the ritual for burial at sea!

As entertainment was at a premium during sea trips, it appeared that most of the off-duty ship's company were on the upper deck looking for all the world like the spectators in those French Revolution movies we use to see; gathered to watch the tumbrel arrive and the aristocrats being led to the guillotine. In fact, on one occasion I was sure I saw the old crone who appeared in all those scenes, knitting and cackling obscenely through blackened, gapped teeth. I never saw the '*Scarlet Pimpernel*' as I believe by that time Leslie Howard had been killed. We had to mount a series of steps and ladders in order to enter our flying domain. First an iron ship's ladder from the upper deck to the platform outside our caboose, then a vertical iron rungged ladder to the catapult deck, and finally a wooden extension ladder from this deck to the aircraft. I refused to count any of these steps just in case one or all of them had thirteen treads.

Upon entering the aircraft, I immediately departed towards the rear where I could turn white unobserved, sat down facing forward and with a nice sturdy back on the seat, relaxed somewhat. In front of me was the radio equipment with its two transmitter coils about the size as present-day large juice cans; the receiver again with its two plug-in coils. Both the receiver and the transmitter were suspended on elastic cords to reduce vibration and also to scare the operator. You learn one absolute law of physics absolutely when you are catapulted off a ship - that is the **Law Of Inertia**, that a body at rest tends to remain at rest; and that for each action there is an equal and opposite reaction. When the aircraft accelerates, anything loose tends to stay where it is - anything fixed in the aircraft (like someone sitting in a seat with a firm back) hurtles towards this stationery object. At some juncture, these two bodies will meet - sooner rather than later, and with considerable pain for one of them.

The generator, which was originally on my desk at my left side and not strapped down, came off the desk to the end of the line, bent the plug and hit me on the shoulder. I spent most of that trip muttering to myself, trying to straighten out the pins on the generator plug and re-tune the transmitter without breaking radio silence. Nothing was ever loose again. I even went so far as to tie the observer in his seat.

The actors and spectators in this launch went their separate ways for a space of three and a half hours at which time the aircraft was to return.

Second Act --- or *What Goes Up Must Come Down*

The method of recovery of the aircraft was to land in the sea, taxi alongside the ship, hook on to the crane and then be hoisted inboard. This sounds easy as assembling a child's toy on Christmas eve. However, as you all know, the instructions always have a few items missing.

As the aircraft approached, the ship - which at this time was steaming ninety degrees out of the wind, turned hard to starboard and headed into the wind. This action created a *'slick'* or smoothing of the water at the stern. The pilot hopefully seizing the opportunity, landed in this slick and of course, into the wind. Now the fun began. The Air Gunner got out of the cockpit and immediately the hatch was closed and the engine revved up and we started to chase the ship. The instructions forgot to mention that the ship did not stop. It did however, as a sop to the aircraft crew, reduce speed - a little.

The Air Gunner climbed up and sat on the upper wing. In his left hand, he clutched the "**D**" ring of the wire slings which he was to attach to the crane hook, his legs were wrapped around as much, and or as many, struts and bracing wires as he could; he was leaning as far forward as possible and busily engaged in prayer!

The reason for this were twofold. If by some chance, he did not hold on firmly to the "**D**" ring, he could fall forward into the sea. If not firmly anchored by his feet he could conceivably fall backward where he'd be hit by the propeller behind him and fall as sliced salami into the sea. Neither prospect held any great attraction for the participant, but appeared to be awaited with bated breath by the *'French Revolutionists'* now lining the guard rails and other points on the ship's upper deck.

The instructions failed to mention that the slick did not last long, and we were approaching the crane and the boom which was amidships under increasingly turbulent sea conditions, created in part of course, by the bow wave of the ship.

BOOM! Boom? I didn't see that in the instructions, but the chunk of wood was an essential part of the recovery procedure at sea. The boom was swung out just about thirty feet ahead of the crane. Attached to the boom was a hawser, to which the Observer secured the nose of the aircraft and then with judicious use of the throttle and handling of the bow line by the ship's crew, the aircraft was plumbed under the crane. The Air Gunner of course, viewed this operation with some alarm. If the boom was approached too rapidly, there were two dangers.

1. The boom could pass over the upper wing on which he was perched and push him violently into the propeller.
2. Alternately he could duck and then find the next wave that lifted the aircraft and boom, acting as a sledge hammer, had made him a '*squishy*' part of the upper wing.

However, all has gone well. We have now jockeyed into position under the crane. It has to be understood that it is extremely difficult for the operator to handle the crane with its heavy ball in a sufficiently delicate fashion as to enable anyone short of Superman to easily hook on. In order to reduce the qualifications for Air Gunners - i.e. that it not be necessary for them to be able to leap tall buildings, a modification was made.

The snatch hook to which you attached the "**D**" ring was controlled by two light gauge steel wires which passed through guides on the ball at the end of the main crane cable. These cables were under the hand control of two seamen on the upper deck adjacent to the crane. More importantly, if the Air Gunner missed catching the hook, it could have then hit the propeller which would tend to affect the aircraft's maneuverability. So if the hook was missed, the seamen pulled on the lines and rapidly raised it. You then reduced power and dropped back to make another attempt.

All this time, the ship had to maintain course and constant speed and if there were enemy subs in the vicinity; she was a sitting duck. Your realization that in all possibility you may be located immediately above the spot where a torpedo could arrive, improved your concentration, ensuring the hook was very rarely missed.

You now became busier than a one-armed paper hanger in a wind storm. First, you hooked on to the slings on the upper mainplane; removed a pin in the hook so you could release the aircraft in case you started to paravane when the crane commenced hoisting. You signaled with one of your spare arms that you had secured the hook. The seamen hauled taut on the lines and the crane operator dropped the weighted snatch mechanism and hopefully there was a successful mating of the male and female portions of the gear. You hoped that the seamen on the upper deck were holding tight and that all downward momentum halted above you, or the odd occasion with new members of the aircraft handling party on the lines - your head restrained the downward passage and you became a little annoyed with the idiot line handlers.

Now, if you had not paravaned (there's that word again) and therefore being hoisted correctly, you passed down two handling lines which were attached to the aircraft and were used by handling party on the upper deck to restrain the aircraft's movement relative to the side of the ship. There were also two other people who had a most fascinating but on most occasions, a very boring job. They were equipped with bamboo poles about 20 feet long and with a sponge end; they looked somewhat like large Polo mallets and were used to keep portions of the aircraft away from the ship's side. I must tell on some other occasion when the personnel handling these were attacked by the aircraft and one of them finished up in the bakery and I never saw the other guy again. I think he asked for another posting.

At any rate, we were hoisted aboard, swung over and lowered on to the catapult and lived happily ever after. It is a matter of interest that it had probably taken you as long to read about the recovery procedure as it did to actually execute it.

HOW THE SENIOR SERVICE DOES IT
or - We'll Show the Air Force

During the course of many moves, I have lost my Log Book along with other mementos and in consequence, I am unable to pin down the precise date. It was a couple of months after the German attack on Russia, as we were one of the first Murmansk convoys.

On this occasion, the crew were Lieutenant Franklin (Pilot), Sub Lieutenant Walker RNVR (Observer) and myself. The **SHROPSHIRE** had been providing escort for a convoy to Murmansk and among the ships in the convoy was an aircraft carrier *HMS ARGUS*, delivering Hurricane fighters to Russia.

The majority of these planes were stored in the hangar below the flight deck, necessitating the removal of their wings in order to get them down the elevator. Aircraft operating from carriers had wings which folded. The Air Force fighters were normal land based planes. The planes had to be flown off upon approaching Murmansk, so there was a group of Royal Air Force mechanics aboard to re-assemble the aircraft as they were brought up to the flight deck. This operation was conducted in short order, something over two hours.

Prinz Eugen

On the return trip to the UK with a convoy including of course, the *ARGUS*, there was the indication that the German cruiser **PRINZ EUGEN** was in the vicinity. It was decided therefore to send the Walrus on a reconnaissance sweep to see if anything could be found.

As usual, there was the usual plethora of data, facts and information passed to the Air Gunner - **NOTHING**! Sitting at the rear of the aircraft in front of the radio with no view of the '*wild blue yonder*' you felt like a mushroom - kept in the dark and fed a load of bullshit. As far as I can recall, we did not even have Gosport tubes (this was a primitive voice pipe). Also, to add to my concern, was the fact that on catapulting, the sea had looked too rough for landing. Surprise! We landed on the *ARGUS*.

Now why should I be surprised you may wonder - we were a naval aircraft, why should it not land on an aircraft carrier.

For one thing, although the Walrus was primarily an amphibian - that is could land on either land or water, whilst engaged in operations from the ship, the wheels were removed to reduce weight, and I had no idea that they had been re-installed prior to take off. Also, the normal method of slowing down an aircraft landing on a carrier flight deck was by means of arrester wires which caught the arrester hook on the tail section of the aircraft. The Walrus has no arrester hook. The pilot can of course, use the air operated brakes if the air bottle adjacent to the Wireless Operator's seat has the valve open - it didn't. The *'mushroom'* in the rear was alerted and rapidly rectified the situation.

We were fortunate in one or two respects. One – the Walrus as I've stated previously, had no pretensions to speed, and in consequence could approach at about 65 knots or roughly 100 feet per second. The carrier was probably doing 30 knots and say a wind speed of 10 knots, our relative speed was only 40 feet per second; a speed that corresponds about 8.5 seconds for the 100 meters - nothing earth shattering.

The most important part of our salvation however, was the bridge. The **ARGUS** was one of, if not the first, aircraft carrier in the Royal Navy and did not have an island bridge on the starboard side as all carriers now do. It had a bridge which was raised and lowered hydraulically, athwart the flight deck. We stopped by gently bumping into it. So we landed and were taken down into the hangar.

> The next day we anchored in Iceland. If the Royal Air Force ground crews were stunned at our landing tactics, we should have told them: *'You ain't seen nothing yet.'*

The normal way of getting airborne whilst in harbor was to hoist the aircraft over the side by means of a crane. The engine, which incidentally had to be started by cranking up a flywheel in the nacelle, engaging a clutch which turned the engine over and simultaneously hand-cranking the generator. As soon as the engine fired, the pilot switched over to the engine-operated generator.

The cranking etc. was usually done by the *'Mushroom'* who sincerely hoped it fired the first time. He would always remember dangling from the crane alongside a jetty in Durban one Sunday morning whilst what appeared to him to be the whole population of the city in their *'Sunday-go-to-meeting'* finery promenaded past, watching his 20 minute effort to coax some life into the heap of junk and being finally ignominiously hoisted back onto the catapult.

The engine was never started until you were hoisted clear of the catapult and on your way over the side. Because it has a pusher type engine and the aircraft was released from the crane about two feet above the water so that the crane, hook, cable etc. would clear the propeller. The reason for this was of course that with the engine running, the aircraft would go ahead and if the crane was still attached, the cable would go back. The result would be a demolished propeller and a fairly irritated pilot.

Now, back to the quarter-deck of **HMS ARGUS**.

I never found out if **ARGUS** had a crane on her flight deck, but it did have one on its quarter-deck and access to the quarter-deck was available from the hangar. As you may or may not be aware, the quarter-deck on a carrier was under the rounddown or rear of the flight deck, thus limiting headroom. We now have an aircraft on the quarter-deck of the carrier and it has to be juggled around until its lifting sings are plumb under the crane hook so we don't drag the plane sideways when we start to hoist. We only have a few inches of headroom; so little in fact that the guardrails have to be dismantled so that we can be swung over the side. Needless to say, this all took some time (it felt like years) but we had a fascinated Air Force audience. Finally however, we were secured to the crane and climbed to our respective places. The pilot and Observer in the cockpit, and the *'Mushroom'* alongside the engine nacelle between the upper and lower wings, ready to start up.

The crane operator, being from the Seaman branch, was now prepared to show these RAF spectators that the Real Navy; as opposed to those poor bloody flying types; knew how to get things done in a hurry. Perhaps he was just fed up with hanging around. He immediately commenced to lifting the aircraft and with a view to putting us over the side, started to swing across the deck and lower us into the water. I, in the meantime, am frantically turning the handle to get the inertia starter up to speed, then turning the hand magneto and pulling the clutch and the engine to fire. It is a race against time and the relentless crane operator.

On the **SHROPSHIRE**, the crane operator and the aircraft handling party have performed this operation many times. Also on the **SHROPSHIRE**, the catapult on which the aircraft rests, is approximately 36 feet above the water. From this quarter-deck to sea level is only about 12 feet. The crane operator on the **SHROPSHIRE** knows I have to start the engine, hand the crank to the observer in the cockpit, climb up to the upper wing, pull the locking pin out to activate the quick release hook, and to stop lowering when the plane is about two feet above surface of the sea.

Unfortunately, this crane operator does not know all or any of the above, and my success in starting the engine has eliminated the possibility of two '*Mushrooms*' having voice communication. So our craft reaches sea level.

Now with the aircraft engine running as soon as we reach sea level, the aircraft wants to taxi and instead of being turned so that we are parallel to the ship, we have established a course away from the ship. Not only that, but we are still hooked on to the crane with me pulling desperately on the crane cable as it threatens to interfere somewhat with the propeller. Fortunately - or unfortunately - as the crane operator realizes there is something amiss and commences to hoist us up again. In order to achieve this, he has to drag us bodily backward through the water until we start to rise. At this point, due to the law of inertia, we continue to travel backwards and then of course, start to swing forward following gravitational laws. Even as a child I was not too fond of uncontrollable swings, so I viewed this performance with a certain dismay. By this time, I had succeeded in removing the locking pin and was in a position to drop the aircraft into the water free from crane obstacle if I could get the right moment. It was not to be.

By now, the crane operator (and I use this term for want of a better one) had decided that a swinging aircraft is dangerous, and again drops us into the sea. Again we go ahead, once more I play with crane cable, again the operator starts to hoist & back we go and of course; once more we swing.

This time I am more prepared and more determined than ever to foil this dastardly attempt to keep us attached to this loathsome ship with its semi-demented crane operator. So, on one of the swings when I felt we were more or less plumb under the crane and the aircraft tail was clear of the ship, I pulled the quick release and we dropped into the water. As we pulled away from *ARGUS* I do believe there was a small cheer from the ranks of the Air Force personnel - those, that is, who were not holding their sides with laughter. I, of course, with usual nonchalance, was waving good-bye to the *ARGUS* with one or two fingers.

There is a footnote to this. I was in a pub some nights later and heard the tail end of a conversation between two RAF types and I'm sure I heard one of them say:

'*I tell you it's true! I was there. They attach them to a crane, get them swinging, then throw them in the water!*'

Ah well, maybe he was discussing some other event. Nevertheless it took almost as long for **HMS ARGUS** to get rid of one Naval aircraft as it did to fly off 24 RAF fighters!

Shortly before the incident mentioned last month, we had just returned from the fleshpots of South Africa; you could hardly describe Capetown in wartime as a hardship posting. And of course as is normal, on return home you go home. Home for 700 Squadron was an aerodome in the Orkney Islands just adjacent to Scapa Flow where most of the females were ewes - but that's another story.

Being at a home base, we were engaged in some training such as night navigation exercises, circuits and bumps, radio work etc. One of the exercises was that we were to carry out, a dummy depth charge attack against a submarine. So one morning, about 0900, sorry - make that 0930; we took off with our full load of two dummy depth charges. Out to the exercise area we fly. As I have stated, my view of either sky, sea or land

was somewhat restricted and there was also a certain lack of communication. Suddenly I heard:
 '*Reel in the trailing aerial.*'

This I did, and we immediately landed in the sea and a not too gentle landing either! I hurried forward and saw a plane had crashed. There was a survivor, and I went to the rear hatch and opened it. As he came alongside, I managed to grab him and haul him into the cockpit. To this day, I am nor sure how it was done. The hatch was only about two feet in diameter, he was waterlogged and with a badly damaged arm, and I was mainly in the 97 pound weakling class. At any rate, we had him safely out of the water.

He was the pilot of an Albacore whose squadron was carrying out dummy torpedo attacks on the area safety ship. The aircraft had sunk with the air gunner and observer in it. The rest of the squadron were circling, but after we arrived, they took off for the aerodome. They boat now approached us and lowered a boat to which we transferred the pilot. We were asked if we could take off. Our pilot said we could, and away they went. By now I am looking around and the sea does seem rough, and all too soon the safety boat disappeared - and we were alone.

I wish the ship had stayed, because as soon as we tried to take off, it was discovered that the sea was indeed rough and if we went any faster, we would probably start shipping water. We were all gathered in the front cockpit and debating what to do. We could not see anything - neither ships nor land. We could of course try to taxi back in. The '*Mushrooms*' suggestion that we fasten the parachutes between the upper and lower wings and sail back did not receive whole-hearted support. It was decided we would have a cigarette break and think some more.

It was in this pensive mood that we suddenly spotted a periscope off our starboard wing and watched in fascination, with our heads rotating in slow motion and with bated breath, as it circled us. I can remember with tremendous clarity, it moved in a counter-clockwise direction from starboard to port and back.

It began blowing its ballast tanks and the conning tower emerged. A figure appeared on the bridge. A shout rang out, and with the normal Englishman's command of foreign languages, we were sure it was German. I think I might have said something like '*Oh brother.*' The pilot probably said '*Dash it all.*' He was an ex-Flag Lieutenant (Lt Franklin RN, *DSC*, *CROIX de GUERRE*). Some few seconds later, all was well with the appearance of an English Signalman and a:
 '*Whip up, Mate? Stuck are you?*'

You guessed it - this was the sub we were supposed to be exercising with. It was Dutch, and so the language difficulty.

I suppose you are wondering how we arranged to get back to the Orkneys. We were towed by the submarine but did manage to persuade them not to take us back through Scapa Flow and to relinquish the tow as soon as we got into calmer water. I hesitate to think what would have happened if we had been paraded past the fleet. Further, the **ARGUS** might have been in port with all those Air Force Types. Imagine what more I might have overheard in the pub;
 '*Not only that, but they being em' back with a submarine.*'

Incidentally, I heard later from the ship's Chaplain after Lt. Franklin had left the **SHROPSHIRE** that he received a Mention In Dispatches for this rescue.

AWARDS AND HONOURS

There is a funny addendum to this incident. As I said, Lt. Franklin had to be very well connected socially to be a Flag Lieutenant, and have these medals which he gained in Norway and I suppose France in early 1940. I presume this because it was in late 1940 when I joined the ship in Capetown and he had them then. This fact led to an event at Wynberg Aerodome in Cape Province. I had been awarded a medal for service in Palestine in 1938, but as yet I had not actually received it. It is now three years later in South Africa.

As is well known, the British Services were reluctant to award medals, and it is very rare indeed to see a serviceman during the war and particularly at this early date with even one medal let alone three - two of which were gallantry awards. In consequence Lt. Franklin was an object of awe to a lot of the South African pilots in training at Wynberg. Well, it had to happen. I was running through the hangar one day and there was the Lieutenant talking to three or four new pilot trainees. I was dressed, immaculate as usual, in dirty old overalls and on my way to tea break.

Lt. Franklin was at one side of the hangar with his normal coterie of novice pilots. He gestured toward me and called:
   "Ah! O'Shaughnasy; just a moment, would you?"

Did he expect me to say:
   "No, I'm in a hurry?"

I trotted over to the group and said,
   "Yes Sir, what do you want?"

   "I have something here for you from the King."
he said; put his hand into his pocket and handed me a small box.

I opened it and saw it was the **Palestine Service Medal**, scanned it briefly, saw my name had been spelt correctly, and shoved it my pocket and politely said,
   "Thank you very much, Sir."

and dashed off to get my tea and bun.

Lt. Franklin told me later I had made his whole day. The eyes of all the new pilots had opened and stood out like organ stops. They had no idea what the medal was and he didn't enlighten them. The casual manner in which we had both treated this incident and his actual medals had them sure that we were so used to getting them that it had become boring. See how myths are created.

TALL TALES FROM THE CAPE
or - Take a Break from Planes

In order to avoid the onset of air sickness in the reader, I thought I should perhaps at this juncture, have a couple of stories which do not concern aircraft.

First of all, let me describe the geography in the vicinity of the Cape of Good Hope, which incidentally is not the most southern tip of Africa. Cape Agulhas that distinction and it is some 100 miles or so further east. Capetown is the last town on the Atlantic side of the isthmus terminating in the Cape of Good Hope. Once around the Cape you are in False Bay, named presumably by some ancient mariner who thought he was round the tip of Africa and into the Indian Ocean. There were a lot of whales harpooned in False Bay in the early 1900's but none had been seen for over 30 years.

Simonstown, the Naval Dockyard town some 20 miles south of Capetown, is located on False Bay. The harbour itself, about 1,400 feet long and about 300 feet wide, had its entrance protected by a submarine net and was about 90 feet wide. This boom and net were pulled back to enable ships to enter or leave. Its purpose was unclear, as at the time I do not believe Italians had made use of their *'Frogmen'* which they used with great success later in Alexandria. At the time of the story neither the Japanese nor the Americans were yet in the war.

Sometime, I believe just after Christmas 1940 or mid-summer (in the Southern Hemisphere) an American Navy cruiser, **USS LOUISVILLE**, arrived in Simonstown to pick up gold. In those days it was dug up in South Africa and buried in Fort Knox. This ship was berthed alongside the jetty on one side and **HMS SHROPSHIRE** was across the harbour on the other. When it came time for the American ship to leave, the boom had to be opened. This was done by two dockyard workmen going out to the boom in a rowboat, pulling out the locking pins in the centre and then the net was hauled in two sections, one to each side of the entrance.

Meanwhile the crew of **SHROPSHIRE** or at least those who couldn't avoid the duty, were painting ship. It was a glorious day - sun shining, hot, the water like a millpond. The ship's company were over the side on catamarans, boson's chairs, slung on scaffolds - all painting, chipping and wire brushing.

We watched the American ship depart through the entrance to the harbour, the boom was hauled back and the locking pins inserted. The scene was one of peace and tranquillity particularly to the Fleet Air Arm contingent who had nothing to do but observe. Suddenly the serenity was shattered. An extremely large sea creature suddenly surfaced and blew in the harbour. The first whale in False Bay for more than thirty years announced his presence. It appeared to be about sixty foot long but from the immediate reaction of the majority of spectators, quite a few of whom were as sea level, it could have been six hundred. It seemed to fill the entire harbour. The ship lost the greater part of its paint stores in about two seconds! Paint cans, brushes, scrapers and wire brushes were immediately dropped by any of the hands who were over the side.

In the next instant, this mob turned into a boarding party and appeared on the upper deck. I have never seen such fast vertical travel in my life! There is no doubt they were direct descendants of Drake and Nelson. You'd have thought the **SHROPSHIRE** was a Prize Ship which had to be captured. People climbed hand over hand up the ropes, hauled the staging and bosun's chairs up like high speed elevators and I feel sure the people from the catamarans in the water simply walked up the ship's side. The whale, apparently fascinated by people's reaction to his appearance and, not wishing to miss the action, seemed to surface with amazing rapidity.

We must not forget to two dockyard workers in their dinghy, rowing back from the boom and heading for stairs in the far corner of the harbour. The whale's effect on them was, if possible, even more startling. You have never seen speed in the water until you a dinghy with two men rowing; the oars seeming to act as legs and the hull apparently out of the water, walking on these legs. Then to see the oars, boat and crew all run up the stairs to the jetty together - it was hard to believe. The Naval Authorities eventually found a descendant of Captain Ahab who approached the boom from seaward, removed the pin, and the boom was drawn back. A couple of hand grenades herded the whale towards the harbour exit and he returned to the solitude of the ocean.

Another whale, which we quite literally ran into in the Denmark Strait, was not so fortunate. It remained wedged on our bow for a day or so and when we anchored in a bay that held a whaling factory, he drifted off the bow and was picked up by the factory and transformed into whatever they make out of whales. Incidentally, I was walking on the fo'cs'le shortly after we had anchored and prior to the whale being towed away. I did not know it was there but what appeared to be a large black and white speckled object was in the water just off the bow. I showed my ignorance by saying,
    "Boy! We really anchored close to that rock, didn't we?"

It was the whale's underside I had seen. You can appreciate why I never got too close to whales at any time.

CHAPTER 16

There Were Pigs in India

"Buddy Breathing" With a Pig?

By Sharkhunters Member Bill Rooney

Members of Garth Doyle's crew *"Sir Tropfrepus"* when in China, got the idea of buying a pig from one of the farmers who could be found on the roadways in Hsinching hauling this item of livestock to the village in their wheelbarrows. Members of the crew bargained with this farmer using, in addition to Chinese paper money, a commodity much more valuable – cigarettes. The transaction was completed and the pig hauled off to the plane. It was decided to stash the pig, properly trussed up, in the rear unpressurized section by the putt-putt (the APU or auxiliary power unit). This particular porker weighed between 200 and 300 pounds. The crew used ropes to haul him through the rear access door, which was seven to eight feet off the ground. Crewmembers used the five or six rung ladder. Needless to say, the pig was uncooperative and engaged in plenty of kicking and snorting.

After takeoff and reaching altitude, one of the crew observed the critter through the window in the bulkhead door and noticed that it wasn't breathing in a healthy pig manner. Garth advised the crew that they had a lot of yen and rupees invested in the pig in addition to many packs of cigarettes, and they better get the pig inside the pressurized area. Meanwhile, due to some mechanical malfunction, flight Engineer Kloster reported difficulty in maintaining cabin pressure at the 8,000 feet equivalent. Accordingly, crewmembers were advised to don their oxygen masks – but what about the pig? Doyle reminded his crew of their investment which he didn't intend to lose. Reluctantly, crewmembers had to share their oxygen with the pig, switching a mask from crewmember to pig, resulting in a joke that went

"One for me, one for the pig. One for me, one for the pig!"

The crew used the phrase as their inside joke long after the event.

The "*One for me, one for the pig*" drill lasted for almost four hours of the six hour long flight across the *Hump*. According to Kloster, the pig kicked loose and had to be rounded up and trussed down again.

Upon landing in Chakulia, they found some former farm boys in the squadron to help unload the pig. However, the Flight Surgeon determined that the pig was unfit for human consumption and condemned it. However, these orders were circumvented and the pig was eaten anyhow, but was served only to the officers however, the Flight Engineer says it was served to all at the 4th of July barbeque.

And what thanks did the crew of *Sir Tropfrepus* get for their adventure, with probably the only pig to touch down in India? We must remember that pigs are not known to hold back their bodily functions, especially when under stress such as making a flight over the *Hump* and being wrestled off the plane.

CHAPTER 17

AICHI M6A Seiran

The Mountain Haze

Seiran was the Japanese for 'Mountain Haze' but this was a submarine-borne attack bomber built by Aichi Kokuki K.K. at Eitoku. This was a single-engine attack bomber with detachable floats, metal construction but fabric control surfaces to save weight and powered by a single Aichi AEIP Atsuta model 30 or model 31 twelve-cylinder inverted-V liquid cooled engine of 1,290, hp which drove a constant pitch three-blade metal propeller. With her crew of two (seated in tandem) this aircraft mounted one rear-firing 13mm Type 2 machine gun and carried two 550 pound bombs or one bomb of about 1,800 pounds.

The M6A had the particular distinction of being the only submarine-borne aircraft to have been built as primarily an offensive weapon. ***SURCOUF***, the giant French submarine, was originally equipped with a reconnaissance aircraft but this was removed early on. The Japanese

Navy included a request for 1,800 submarines of the *I-400* Class. Each of these boats displaced 4,500 tons, and each was to be equipped with a large watertight hangar capable of accommodating two of these attack aircraft, to be launched by a catapult on the forward deck.

First of the Class, this is *I-400*

However, more conventional submarines being of a higher priority, the revised *'Fourth Reinforcement Program'* was scaled down to an order of only 5 of these submarines to be equipped with the enlarged hangar to accommodate three aircraft.

The hangar was to measure only 11 ½ feet in diameter and was situated slightly to starboard of the centerline and near deck level. It was too cramped for an aircraft with a radial air-cooled engine, hence the in-line V was selected as the engine could be warmed up while still in the hangar.

In 1942, Aichi was instructed to design a navy experimental 17-Shi special attack bomber for use aboard these submarines. The original specifications called for a fast catapult-launched aircraft without undercarriage. However, this decision later changed to accommodate detachable twin floats. There were two versions of the aircraft – the M6A1 Seiran with detachable floats, intended for attack missions, and the trainer version M6A1-K (Seiran Kai) with retractable undercarriage.

The first prototype of the M6A1 was completed in November 1943, and was powered by a 1,400 hp Aichi AE1P Atsuta 30 twelve-cylinder inverted v liquid cooled engine. The plane was characterized by a complicated wing and tail folding system. The wings swiveled on their rear spar to lie flat along the fuselage, the tip of the vertical tail sections folded to starboard, and the horizontal tail sections forward. Basically, the wings folded like those of a butterfly in a cocoon. Despite the apparent complexity of the folding systems and the lack of space aboard the *I-400* Class submarines, it could be readier for flight in less than seven minutes by the four man ground crew. Fluorescent paint was used on all the important sections of the aircraft to help in nighttime assembly.

The Japanese Navy laid plans for an attack on the lock gates of the Panama Canal by the 1st Submarine Flotilla, made up of *I-400* and *I-401;* large submarines, each carrying three M6A1 Seiran attack bombers, and the pair would be backed up by *I-13* and *I-14* which would carry two Seiran aircraft. However, the target was changed to the U.S. Navy anchorage at Ulithi Atoll and the 1st Submarine Flotilla headed to sea in late July 1945 but the war ended before they could carry out any attacks.

EDITOR NOTE – A Japanese contributor told us that this was like rushing to put out a fire on the horizon when your own kimono was blazing. As a side note, the commander of *I-400* was the notorious Ariizumi '*the Butcher*'. Some of his many atrocities when commanding *I-8* were covered in our previous book *"U-Boat!"* volume 2 currently available from Sharkhunters.

CHAPTER 18

Both Sides of the Same Coin

The Colin Kelly Story

Colin Kelly was the first American hero of World War Two. He is credited with single-handedly attacking and sinking the Japanese battleship **HARUNA** (seen here) and he was highly decorated for this, posthumously. The United States was being beaten at every

turn and the US needed a hero. Colin Kelly filled the bill and he was reported to the American public as the brave young American pilot who, against all odds, sank the I.J.N. battleship **HARUNA**. It was a great patriotic and heart wrenching story because Kelly was killed in this heroic deed. Problem – this was all propaganda.

.....as remembered by one of Kelly's crew and reported by the American press;

On the morning of 10 December 1941, six B-17 Flying Fortresses sat in the rain at a rough landing strip on the Philippine Island of Luzon. The crews had spent the night without food, sleeping in or under their planes. Of the war situation, which had begun for the United States just three days before, they knew nothing but Japan had attacked Clark Field near Manila.

Squad Commanding Officer Emmett *'Rosy'* O'Donell, Jr. had flown to Clark before daylight to get orders for his squadron. He radioed his pilots to proceed to Clark at daybreak, but only 3 of the *'Forts'* were allowed to land. They were flown by Captain Colin P. Kelly, Jr., Lt. Schaetzel and Lt. Montgomery. Kelly, a graduate of West Point and former B-17 instructor, was one of the most experienced pilots of the Bomb Group.

An imminent air attack sent the three bombers off to their respective targets before refueling and bomb loadings were completed. Captain Kelly had only three 600 pound bombs aboard and orders to attack airfields on Formosa, some 500 miles north of Clark. Their mission would earn Kelly a place in American history and legend.

In the confusion of the early days of Pacific war, Kelly was credited with sinking a Japanese battleship and with the award of the Medal of Honor. Overnight he became a national hero. It was later determined that Kelly and his crew did not sink a battleship nor was he awarded the Medal of Honor, although some still believe both. In fact, he was recommended for the Medal of Honor but rather, he received the Distinguished Service Cross on orders of General Douglas MacArthur's headquarters.

For Captain Kelly it was a solo mission deep into territory where the Japanese held absolute air superiority – and they had no fighter escort. By 10 December, there were only twenty-two flyable P-40 fighters and a few obsolete P-35 fighters left. As they flew north toward Formosa, Kelly and his crew passed over a large Japanese landing in progress at Apari on the north coast of Luzon. The presence of an enemy carrier in the vicinity had also been reported.

Kelly radioed Clark Field for permission to attack the landing force, which was supported by several destroyers and a large warship thought to be a battleship which was bombarding the coast from several miles offshore. After two calls to Clark that brought only a response to stand by, Kelly told the crew they were going ahead on his decision to attack the battleship – which was actually a cruiser. Kelly made two dry runs at 20,000 feet, giving his bombardier, Sgt. Levin, time to set up for an accurate drop.

On his third run, he told Levin to release the bombs in train. As best the crew could remember, two of the three bombs bracketed the ship with one direct hit. Smoke prevented more accurate assessment. The B-17 then headed for Clark Field with an empty bomb bay. As the B-17 approached Clark Field, it was jumped by enemy fighters.

The first attack killed TSgt. Delehanty, wounded Pfc. Robert Altman and destroyed the instrument panel. A second attack set the left wing on fire. This fire quickly spread into the fuselage, filling the flight deck with dense smoke.

Captain Kelly ordered the crew to bail out while he still had control of the doomed bomber. Fire as well as smoke began to engulf the fire deck. Sgt. Halkyard, Pfc. Money and Pfc. Altman went out the rear. Lt. Bean and Sgt. Levin fought to pry open a stuck escape hatch and finally got out of the bomber, and hit the silk.

The nose of the aircraft was an inferno. Colin Kelly remained at the controls as copilot Lt. Don Robins moved to the upper escape hatch. At that moment, the plane exploded, hurling a badly burned Lt. Robins clear of the aircraft.

The B-17 crashed about 5 miles from Clark Field and Colin Kelly's body was found nearby. The early report of his heroism, which was an inspiration to a nation in the shock of war, is in no way diminished by the actual events of that December day in 1941. Alone and far from friendly territory, he attacked and damaged a heavily armed ship, then sacrificed his own life to save his crew.

...........as remembered by Japanese fighter Ace Saburo Sakai;

"The third day of the war with America is one I will long remember for on 10 December, I shot down my first Boeing B-17. After the war, I found that this particular bomber was piloted by Captain Colin Kelly, an American air hero.

Twenty-seven of our fighters circled over Clark Field, but we found not a single target. We then turned north to fly cover for the Japanese convoy landing troops at Vigan. One light cruiser of the 4,000 ton *NAGARA* type and six destroyers escorted four transports. An American account of this force, based on reports of the surviving crew of Captain Kelly's plane, grossly exaggerated the number of ships. According to the Americans, our force comprised the battleship *HARUNA* of 29,000 tons, six cruisers, ten destroyers and between 15 and 20 troop transports.

While maintaining cover over the transports at 18,000 feet, I noticed three large water rings (explosions) near the ships. None were hit, although the American report of the attack claimed that the nonexistent battleship had received one direct hit and two near misses, and was left smoking and trailing oil. I saw a lone B-17, about 6,000 feet above us, speed southward. We had never heard of unescorted bombers in battle. Unbelievable as it seemed, that B-17 made a lone attack in the very teeth of our planes. That pilot certainly did not lack courage.

The B-17 was surprisingly fast, and only under full throttle did we manage to get within attacking distance. This was our first experience with a B-17 and the airplane's unusual size caused us to misjudge our distance. All through the attack, the Fortress kept up a steady stream of fire at us from its gun positions.

After my pass, I noticed that we were over Clark Field. I decided to try a close-in attack directly from the rear, knowing that the early B-17 models lacked tail turrets. Under full throttle, I swung in behind the bomber and closed in for firing.

The guns of the Fortress flashed brightly as the pilot fish-tailed from side to side, trying to give the side gunners the opportunity to catch me in their sights. I moved in ahead of two fighters and opened fire. Pieces of metal flew off in chunks from the bomber's right wing and then a thin white film sprayed back. It looked like jettisoned gasoline but it might have been smoke. I kept up my fire against the damaged area, hoping to either hit the fuel tanks or oxygen system with my cannon shells. Abruptly the film turned into a geyser. The bomber's guns ceased firing and the plane was afire within the fuselage.

I banked away as the bomber nosed down. Miraculously, its wings were on an even keel and the bomber's pilot might have been trying to crash land on Clark Field. I dove after the crippled Fortress and took pictures with my Leica. At 7,000 feet three men bailed out. Their chutes opened, and then the B-17 disappeared into an overcast.

Later we heard reports that the Americans had damned our fighter pilots for machine gunning the crewmen who drifted to earth. This was pure propaganda. Mine was the only Zero near the bomber, and I had not a single bullet left. No Japanese pilot actually saw the B-17 crash, so credit for the kill was denied at the time.

The bomber pilot's courage in attempting his solo bombing run was the subject of much discussion that night in our billets. The discrepancies of the surviving crew member's reports in no way detracted from this act of heroism."

EDITOR NOTE – Saburo Sakai was a Sharkhunters Member

…………..as remembered in an interview;

Sharkhunters Member Glenn Troelstrup was a radio show host for the military, and here is what he remembers:

"Captain Colin Kelly was one of my boyhood heroes, and I remember an interview I taped with his surviving radio operator, Cpl. Money. He was later commissioned and an Air Force major when, as News Director of Clark AFB, Philippines, we discussed the so-called battleship ***HARUNA*** sinking.

He was frank about exploding the myth. Before I could air the interview on one of my news shows (three times per day) I had to clear it with Headquarters, 13th Air Force, at Clark. My radio station commander, Captain Damon Eccles, delivered the tape to the P.I.O., a colonel, and Headquarters exploded! Eccles was ordered to have me burn the tape, with him at witness – after Headquarters made a copy. Money was admonished for the interview.

I made a studio transcription of the tape before it was destroyed, but the engineer mentioned it to Eccles, who destroyed that himself.

Money described the single-plane mission, with only three heavy bombs, seeking a reported convoy approaching northern Luzon from Formosa (Taiwan), led by the ***HARUNA***. They spotted finally only a single, large unescorted troop transport or cargo ship and scored two near misses, apparently damaging the hull plates and forcing the vessel to head for shallow water and apparently grounding.

Kelly's B-17 was arcing by Mt. Arayat and beginning the landing when the Zero group led by Saburo Sakai attacked. Money said the landing was aborted, and Kelly tried to climb so it could defend itself, and he could gain altitude for possibly abandoning.

To shorten the rest and drop detail, Kelly ordered crew survivors to hit the silk. He was the last to jump, but didn't report in. Searchers couldn't locate him either. Several days later, a rice farmer reported to a Pampanga constable post that the decomposing remains of an airman with an unopened 'chute was in his paddy. It was Kelly.

Money said the survivors weren't machine gunned in the air and neither Kelly's body nor 'chute showed any evidence of being hit by gunfire, but the War Department quickly packaged Kelly (and a few others) as instant heroes, awarded them medals posthumously, and left their largely Pentagon manufactured deeds uncorrected in later years."

CHAPTER 19

Attack on Convoy PQ.18

This convoy was decimated by U-Bootwaffe and Luftwaffe in one of the bloodiest battles in WW II

We begin with the text of a 23 November 1942 memo from the U.S. Naval Attaché at the American embassy in Moscow, USSR to the Chief of Naval Operations entitled:
 'Report of Observations and Activities During Travel with North Russian Convoy from New York to Molotovak, USSR'

The writer is considered a very reliable and mature observer. His letter is believed to be or more than usual interest and value.

The memo is stamped *'CONFIDENTIAL'* and is signed J. H. Dungan.

Here is that memo, dated 17 October 1942 to the Chief of Naval Operations from Ensign John H. Hanshaw:

1. In accordance with orders issued by the Chief of Bureau of Personnel dated 10 May 1942, I departed from Washington DC on 31 May 1942 for New York. Upon arrival there, I reported to the U.S. Dispatch Agency for assignment to a vessel on which to take passage for myself and about 100 tons of supplies for the American Embassy, Moscow. I was advised to report on board the *SS VIRGINIA DARE* at Hoboken, NJ prior to 4 June 1942. On 3 June I reported on board that vessel for passage and to the Commanding Officer of the U.S. Navy Armed Guard for such duties as he may wish to assign me while so traveling.

2. The *VIRGINIA DARE* sailed on the following schedule in company with a convoy of other cargo vessels and escorted by British naval vessels.

3. While at Gunrock, with permission of the U.S. Navy Observer at that port, I visited Glasgow, Edinburgh and London. Enroute from Lock Ewe to Molotovak, we dropped some vessels of the convoy and picked up a few vessels from that port. Our escort from Scotland to Iceland was somewhat heavier than previously. We passed Hvalfjordur, Iceland on 7 September 1942 without stopping. On 9 September 1942 when to the N.E. of Iceland, our escort was increased considerably. One aircraft carrier, small size, converted anti-aircraft cruiser, one sloop, two submarines, four small rescue ships, one heavy cruiser, a few corvettes, destroyers and trawlers comprised the British escort from 9 September until 2200 on 16 September, when the major part of the escorting vessels withdrew to return west. At the same time, three or four Russian destroyers joined our escort. It was felt that the major vessels of the escort should have accompanied the convoy into port as the strongest enemy attack was after they left.

4. The *SS VIRGINIA DARE* is one of the new Liberty Ships, built at Wilmington NC, a welded hull; was on her maiden voyage. While enroute from Philadelphia to Hoboken, she ran aground. Was refloated and most of the cargo discharged there. She was then drydocked and repairs to her bottom were made. Was reloaded and after about ready to sail, the Russian agents came aboard and stated they had orders to discharge the present cargo which consisted mostly of food and miscellaneous cargo. They stated the Soviet Government wanted nothing but war materiel, that although they were short of food, they did not wish cargo space used for anything but necessary war materials. The ship was unloaded and then a cargo of tanks, trucks, crated aircraft, machinery, small arms, ammunition, smokeless powder and about 1,200 tons of TNT taken aboard. The ship was under command of Captain A. L. Johnson and its agents the Moore-McCormack S.S. Company.

5. An Armed Guard crew consisting of the Officer in Charge, Lieutenant John L. Laird and twenty-five enlisted men manned the 4 inch rifle, 3 inch anti-aircraft gun and eight 20mm anti-aircraft guns. While in Scotland, the ship was equipped with a barrage balloon and two P.A.C. wire rockets as well as about six smoke floats. Lieutenant Laird exhibited excellent control over his crew and showed remarkable ability in organizing his gun stations and in preparing his station bills. Regardless of the long tiresome

trip with long stops at Iceland and Loch Ewe where no liberty or recreation was available, the morale of his crew remained excellent and when under heavy attack by the enemy, they all performed their assigned duties in a most excellent and commendable manner. During the eight-day period of emergency, they were required to stand two hour watches on and two off continuously, and at all times when under attack and they were required to be on duty for as long as five to six hours at a time, during which time the weather was extremely cold and wet.

At all times there was excellent relations and cooperation between the merchant marine crew and the Armed Guard crew. It was necessary to use some of the merchant marine crew to assist at the gun stations. This they did most willingly and enthusiastically. As was the case with many of the ships, the Captain was not so very enthusiastic about traveling in convoy due to the danger of collision in fogs and at night when all ships were running without lights. Upon leaving Cape Cod, we encountered extremely heavy fog. The ships of the convoy became separated and went on to Halifax on their own. We arrived there ahead of most of the vessels which came in singly all during the day. The Captain stated that due to not having enough rudder for the size of the ship, it was difficult to properly handle the ship in close formation.

However, it was noted that when under heavy attack, the Commodore of the Convoy had hardly any difficulty in keeping the vessels in their proper positions. In fact it was noted that the officers of the merchant vessels exhibited a great deal more respect for the Naval personnel, and eagerly looked forward to them for maximum protection after the first attack on the convoy. It is my belief however, that should the prohibition of liquor aboard the vessels be rigidly enforced, much better conditions would follow. Under the trying conditions in the attack zones a couple of the officers tried to allay their tenseness and fear by a little overindulgence in liquor.

At 0615, 24 June 1942, the gun crews sighted what they believed to be a submarine periscope on our port quarter. One shot from each the 5" and 4" guns were fired. Results unknown and object not seen again. This occurred just prior to our entry into Sidney, NS (Canada) harbor.

Due to the transfer of the gunner on No. 4, 20m/m. gun, to the hospital in Scotland, the writer asked the Officer in charge of the Armed Guard to be assigned in his place. My offer was gladly accepted and was assigned accordingly.

At 1300 on 12 September 1942, an enemy reconnaissance plane was sighted. General quarters were sounded and all guns manned. Hurricane planes from the escorting carrier took off and pursued the enemy plane, which, however, turned and headed back toward the east. A few shots from the escorting vessels.

At 0735, 13 September 1942, position 8° 54 E x 75° 59 N, enemy aircraft sighted. All guns manned. Planes from carrier pursued them for a distance and then returned to the carrier. Secured about 0800. At 0810 we sighted two disturbances in the water about 1,000 yards off our starboard quarter. Some thought them to be a whale blowing. At about 0815 while still watching for further disturbance of the water, we observed an explosion about amidships of a vessel in the outer column to our starboard beam.

U-Boat Torpedoes a Ship in Convoy PQ.18

The water shot up to about 50 feet in the air with part of the ship or its deck cargo, flying in the air. The ship began to settle and the crew abandoned ship in three life boats. The ship began settling and disappeared in its final dive within 8 minutes. At about 0825 a similar explosion was noted about amidships of a Liberty ship which was in the same column but just astern of the first ship torpedoed. This ship began settling by the head but remained afloat. The crew abandoned ship and a British destroyer fired on the ship and sank it. The survivors of the two ships were picked up by the rescue vessels.

U-405 Dockside prior to Engaging Convoy PQ.18

The first ship appears to have been hit by torpedoes from both *U-405* (Hopmann) and also *U-408* (von Hymmen). The second was the victim of *U-589* (Horrer).

At about 1030 a large number of enemy aircraft were heard above the clouds (ceiling about 500 feet). A large number of bombs were dropped over the entire convoy - four of which straddled our ship, two hitting about 300 feet off out starboard beam and two hitting about the same distance on our port beam. No explosions from these bombs, only very large splashes. At about 1045, a ship which was about 300 feet off our starboard bow was hit by what apparently seemed to be a heavy bomb (the whistling sound of the falling bomb was very loud and seemed to be directly over our head) and the ship exploded and there was a rather loud explosion with one huge mass of flames shooting up into the air. The flames died down and in less than 30 second there remained nothing of the ship except a few pieces of smoking cork or wood no larger than a football.

Ammunition Ship Disintegrates

As the ships were zigzagging, our vessel passed directly over the oil slick where the destroyed vessel was. We felt about 50 or 60 light explosions under our hull and one rather large explosion which was followed by apparently pieces of metal hitting the bottom of our hull. There were no survivors. The ship was a British vessel of about 9000 tons. We did hear someone scream loudly immediately after the explosion.

At about 1055 a submarine's periscope was seen on our port beam. We put helm hard right and a torpedo was seen by the forward gun crews to pass immediately in front of our bow. About 1000 another torpedo apparently launched from the same submarine was seen heading in our general direction but it went 'wild' also. We all fired at the spot where the periscope was seen. Results unknown, but believed that no damage done as no oil slick was observed then. A corvette dropped depth a charge and a small slick of about 75 square feet was observed. It was believed however that it was caused by the depth charge.

Small groups of enemy planes appeared overhead and were fired upon. No bombs dropped during this period. At about 1500, torpedo planes were sighted flying about 100 feet above the water just on the horizon on our starboard bow. All ships commenced firing on them as they came within range. The fire did not seem to distract them as they continued on toward us. As they came nearer they increased their altitude to about 300 to 400 feet. Our guns were firing on them when I observed one flying about 75 feet above the water and apparently heading in so as to get ahead on our starboard beam. I opened fire on it and it began smoking and then started burning. It dropped its torpedoes which went astern of us and it then fell into the sea about 200 feet off our port quarter.

As the Liberty ship just astern of us was torpedoed at about that time some of the gun crew seemed to think one of the torpedoes from that plane hit the Liberty ship. The ship began settling by the stern and remained about half afloat. The crew took to the life boats and were rescued by the rescue ships. The ship was then sunk by a British destroyer. The Liberty ships seemed to have pretty good watertight integrity.

That was possibly the **OLIVER ELLSWORTH**, hit by either *U-589* (Horrer) or *U-408* (von Hymmen)

The planes continued their attack and the escort vessels commenced an intense fire at the planes which had now increased their altitude to about 1000 feet. One plane heading directly at our port bow was destroyed by the gunner on No. 2 forward 20mm gun. Hurricane planes were launched from the carrier and caused the attacking planes to scatter. The planes, as they were scattering, dropped bombs wildly and two cargo vessels on the extreme port side of the convoy were hit. Both began burning. One started settling and sunk while the other after fighting the flames fiercely managed to extinguish the fire and continued afloat. Later she resumed her regular position in the convoy. The attacking planes then scattered seemed to head for their base. The attack lasted about 55 minutes.

At about 1630 another group of about 10 enemy planes were sighted flying low on the horizon, coming in from our starboard bow. By this time the escorting destroyers had formed a ring around the convoy at about a mile off. These vessels set up an intense fire and caused the planes to scatter in all directions.

At about 1700 seven planes made an attempt to attack 'en mass' on the rear of our column. They were dispersed by heavy fire from our vessel and the heavy cruiser just to our port. Some planes were observed to fall into the sea. Three planes were then seen to take more altitude and head for their base. We secured from general quarters and maintained condition II watch. At about 1800, it being twilight, another group of planes appeared. We were unable to determine how many but estimated about 15. The escorting vessels began a heavy fire as well as all the cargo vessels on our side of the convoy. The planes scattered and made individual attacks. The gunner on No. 1 20mm gun got a direct hit and the plane was seen to fall flaming into the sea on our starboard bow. This attack lasted about 35 minutes. We estimated that we had lost 7 ships during the day. Unable to estimate the number of planes shot down. We secured at about 2230. We had light westerly winds and temperature about 30 degrees. A light snow was falling.

At 0400, 14 September 1942 position 75° 57"N x 21 °45"E, a merchant tanker, last ship in column six, was torpedoed by a submarine which hit her near the stern and caused a very large explosion. She remained partly afloat while fiercely burning. A British destroyer eventually had to sink her. This was the 8,992 ton British motor tanker ***ATHELTEMPLAR***, sunk by ***U-457*** commanded by Korvettenkapitän Karl Brandenburg.

At 0800 a reconnaissance plane was observed on starboard beam - out of gun range. Secured from General Quarters after plane disappeared.

At 0900 apparently number of submarines in vicinity as many depth charges dropped around and among the convoy. Apparently one submarine sunk to our starboard as much oil and debris was observed coming to the surface there.

EDITOR NOTE - This was *U-88* commanded by Kapitänleutnant Heino Bohmann sunk by *HMS ONSLOW* (photo below) or *U-589* under command of Kapitänleutnant Hans-Joachim Horrer sunk by *HMS FALKNOR*. Both these U-Boats were sunk in the same area about the same time with all hands lost, so it is unclear which boat the writer of this USN report saw being destroyed.

At 1230 General Quarters sounded. 15 torpedo planes appeared on the horizon flying very low off our starboard bow. Escort vessels which surrounded convoy let loose with a fierce attack on them. They scattered and then came in from directly ahead and from the port of the convoy, flying in pairs. They continued their attack this time on the heavy British cruiser which was the lead ship in the center of the convoy, and the aircraft carrier which was then in a position well aft and to the port side of the convoy.

These two ships so well defended themselves that some of the planes were shot down by them and they continued in their position. However, they had many close calls and we thought many times they had been hit - the bombs were falling so close. We could not tell how close the torpedoes came to them.

As on previous attacks, the planes strafed the ships with machine gun fire at every opportunity. Apparently they did not do much damage with the machine gun fire. We did learn afterwards that some men had been wounded by them.

The planes seemed to *'be on their own'* and began attacks by flying in a *'hedge-hopping'* manner over the convoy. One plane was shot down by the gunner on one of the 20mm forward guns and another completely destroyed when it exploded after being hit by our forward 3" gun, when these planes were coming at us preparatory to launching torpedoes.

A third plane coming at us from a little aft of the port beam was leveling off to launch her torpedoes when I fired practically a full magazine of shells into it thereby causing it to start burning and upset its plan of attack. It apparently tried to gain altitude and tried to go ahead of our bow. I continued firing on it until it crashed head on into the side of the **SS MARY LUCHENBACH**, (photo below) when a terrible explosion occurred completely destroying the plane and the ship.

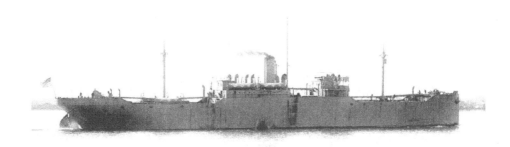

The forward gunners seemed to think that a plane attacking the *MARY LUCHENBACH* from her starboard at the same time may have torpedoed the ship about the time the other plane crashed into it. Apparently both planes were destroyed by the explosion.

The *MARY LUCHENBACH* was in column directly ahead of our ship, about 800 feet but a little out of line to port when she was hit. The explosion was so severe that it threw most of us flat on the deck. As I was firing the gun it seemed to almost mash me into the gun and mount, bruising my right knee quite badly. The fires in our fireroom were extinguished, and the steering gear impaired, the compasses went 'haywire' and slight damage done to various parts of the ship. An armor-piercing shell of about 80mm hit an iron rail on the bridge deck cutting into it and tore a piece of concrete out of the deck. It then fell to a crate on deck. Numerous pieces of metal fell on the ship, including another shell like the one described above, which penetrated a crated airplane on the after deck and the hatch cover of No. 4 hatch finally lodging almost thru the heavy board and within inches of about 400 tons of T.N.T.!

Due to the heavy explosion, it was thought that our hull had been damaged. Soundings were made and it was found no damage had been done.

When the ship exploded, we were so close to it that before the engines could be reversed, our bow was at the edge of the wall of flames. However, as the flames died down within about one minute of the explosion, no damage was done in this respect to our ship. We later were informed that considerable damage was caused to the *SS NATHANIEL GREEN* by the explosion as she, although farther away than our ship, was broadside to the exploded ship.

As we passed thru the debris of the *MARY LUCHENBACH* we noticed the flash of a small light in the water and heard someone calling,
   "Help! Help!"

As we were still under attack and firing, no attempt was made to rescue the man as we observed also, that the rescue ships were heading up that way. It was later learned that the man was a ship's mess boy, colored, that had, while frightened, jumped overboard from the *NATHANIEL GREEN* and was rescued.

The weather became overcast with heavy clouds which probably prevented another night aircraft attack. However, submarines continued to make attempted attacks but due to the excellent patrol of the escorting vessels and their continued dropping of depth charges during the night, apparently no damage was done.

15 September 1942, position 75° 52"N x 35° 27"E. At 0300 the after gun crew reported that a torpedo had just passed under the stern of our ship, coming to the surface at a very fast speed, from our starboard quarter. Six shots from the 20mm guns were fired at a spot where it was believed the submarine may have been. A destroyer over the spot dropping depth charges. Results unknown.

EDITOR NOTE - there were no attacks by U-Boats on this convoy on 15 Sept. Two U-Boats made torpedo attacks on ships of *PQ.18* on the 16th, but hit nothing. Perhaps the gun crews were a bit nervous. Couldn't blame them.

Submarines continued in our vicinity all day but as far as known by us, no ships were hit by them today. At 1500 a large number of bombers began dropping bombs from high altitude - that is - above the clouds. This continued until 1545. Many very near hits were observed throughout the convoy but as far as is known no ships were hit. Two of the bombers chanced at dive bombing and were shot down by vessels of the escort and convoy ships. One came near enough to us to fire on it and it is believed that we put a few shells into it after it was afire. It is believed that the Hurricanes from the carrier did a magnificent job in dispersing the bombers. It was estimated that there were about 10 attacking planes. No further attacks today. Submarines continued in vicinity and destroyers continued dropping depth charges during the day and throughout the night. Weather quite overcast and snow began falling rather heavily.

During the past three days, it had been quite noticeable that the personnel have lost their heavy appetites and complained of not being able to sleep. However, although all very tired and worn after practically three days of

constant tenseness and on the alert, they have now started to keep the cooks busy and all seem to be able to sleep most anyplace. After having seen the way we have been able to defend our own ship they have new confidence that we will be able to continue to keep afloat. However, many have remarked:
   "I wish we would get torpedoed by a submarine."

While this wish was made as all hands have been rather *'on their toes'* because of the 1,200 tons of T.N.T. aboard and especially after seeing what happened to the two ships that exploded right next to us.

16 September 1942: continuing on easterly course off the Spitzbergen Banks. Destroyers continued to drop depth charges all day. At 1900 a torpedo was observed coming to the surface about 300 feet off our port quarter. About 0700 an enemy reconnaissance plane was observed rather high. A few shots were fired by escort vessels and the plane disappeared. Continued snowing. Heavy winds and very cold. At about 2200 a major part of the British escort left us, heading back toward Ireland; a few small Russian destroyers having replaced them. The personnel were quite concerned about this as they believed the full escort should continue into port with us, which is still about 3 days away.

17 September 1942: weather continued cold but snow stopped and weather became clear, sea calm. About 1030 an enemy plane observed on reconnaissance duty. Left in a few minutes. At 1700 another plane, *Ju-88* circled closely over the convoy. Some shots were fired at it as it disappeared into the clouds. Weather became bad again. No submarines noted in vicinity today.

18 September 1942: position 75° 52N x 35° 27E. At 1040, four enemy planes appeared high overhead and began dropping bombs all over the convoy. Then a number of planes attacked by dive-bombing the convoy after which the planes attacked from low level flying by, and dropping torpedoes. The planes headed for us from off our port bow and launched two torpedoes which, due to our increased speed to about ten and one half knots and zig-zagging caused the torpedoes to barely miss our stern.

About two minutes later, another launched another torpedo off our port bow which, while we were zig-zagging, came almost alongside our port quarter at a speed of about 18 or 19 knots. The torpedoes seemed to be about ten to twelve feet long and approximately twelve inches in diameter. At times, it seemed as though the torpedoes were regulated so that if they first missed their target they were able to turn at different angles and even completely in the reverse direction. Others seemed to act almost like a porpoise.

EDITOR NOTE – German U-Boats used many unusual torpedoes including the LUT (Lagen unabhänginger Torpedo) which had a pre-set gyro angle and once inside a convoy, would make zig zag course changes in an attempt to hit anything.

The above attack lasted about one hour. At about 1145 ten low flying planes, some of them four-engine Fokker-Wulff (sic) torpedo planes approached from our port quarter right on the horizon. All ships were fully ready for them and as soon as they were in range and bombing, all hands cut loose on them. The escort vessels really poured a steady stream of fire into them which caused them to break their frontal attack and split up into pairs. Each pair concentrated on apparently a designated ship of the convoy. They seemed to strafe the ships wit machine gun fire while launching torpedoes more heavily than heretofore.

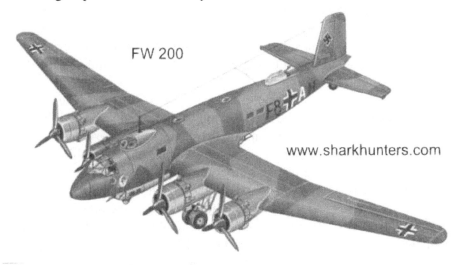

A four engine torpedo plane (apparently a Fokker-Wulff 200) made a pass at our ship and launched her four torpedoes at us from the starboard but due to our zig-zagging, again we were missed. The plane made a heavy right bank and headed up between our column and the column on our port.

The after 20mm guns and my gun immediately began firing on it as it seemed to be suspended momentarily on its side with its top right to us. My gun jammed after 4 shots hit it apparently in the after part of the fuselage. At about the same time, the two after guns had jams and before we had our guns in working order again the plane had gotten out of range.

One of my loaders noticed the gunner in the after turret leaning limply over his gun with his left arm dangling down as if he were dead. Other ships ahead took up the fire on his and as he was smoking some, it is believed that he was one of the planes we later saw burning in the water ahead. We noticed three planes of this attack on our side of the convoy go into the sea aflame.

The Commodore's ship apparently brought down a large four engine, as one crashed almost dead ahead of him, burning fiercely. We noticed a dive-bomber diving on one of the ships on the after port wing of the convoy. There was quite a large explosion and we observed the crew abandoning ship (it was believed to be the **SS KENTUCKY**) and the rescue ship and a destroyer were standing by. It appeared as the ship was not damaged enough to sink and the crew apparently started to return to the ship when two planes suddenly appeared and launched torpedoes at her. She immediately began to settle after being hit and sank within about two minutes.

Today's attacks seemed to be more vicious and more determined than any yet. The attack lasted almost continuously from 1040 to 2400. It seemed that practically every ship had near hits by bombs and many, like us, must have been barely missed by the numerous torpedoes that were launched. The British Hurricane fighter that was carried on a catapult on a British cargo vessel was launched during the hottest part of the attack. He gave chase to a number of the planes and was no doubt responsible for some of them withdrawing. It was learned later that he shot down two planes before he was compelled to head for shore due to the shortage of gas.

This, it seemed, was the most outstanding heroic deed of the whole trip, as the strafing from the planes as well as the intense fire from all ships was so heavy that it did not seem possible that he could be missed.

At about 2300 enemy planes were heard overhead but soon disappeared as it started snowing rather heavily. Also, about this time a few Russian planes appeared on the scene. Total ships lost are 15

19 September, 1942: off Kanin Peninsula. At 1130 a British destroyer carrying survivors cruised up thru the convoy playing *'Little Man, You've Had a Long Day'* on their loudspeaker. On a previous day, right after we had shot down three planes within a few seconds, a British destroyer cruised up near us at high speed and shouted over their loudspeaker:
'Congratulations, excellent shooting."

This little incident of good humor and word of praise lifted the morale of the personnel greatly. At 1700 enemy planes appeared overhead. Five Russian planes appeared and extremely heavy winds and bad weather caused the planes to return to their bases without any attacks being made as far as we could see. The weather became very bad and we were compelled to cruise back and forth all day and night, as unable to head into the shallow harbor. Russian planes constantly patrolling the convoy.

20 September 1942 - still cruising back and forth due to heavy winds and seas. At 1610 we heard enemy planes overhead and observed five heavy time bombs explode among the convoy near the ships directly ahead of us. Russian planes appeared and began attacking the enemy planes. About 1715 another enemy plane appeared over our starboard quarter at a very high altitude. British cruiser fired a few salvos at it. Heavy snow began and plane disappeared. Still unable to go into port due to heave weather.

21 Sep. 1942 - at 0930 took on Russian Naval Officer as pilot and headed into Nolotovok. At 1000 an enemy plane appeared overhead. Some shots were fired. The plane disappeared; apparently back to its base. At 1657 we moored to the key at Nolotovok. Discharge of cargo commenced immediately with Russian prison labor. At 2200 enemy planes appeared over head. All hands to General Quarters, but no shots fired as the planes appeared to have gone on over toward Archanglesk. The Russian shore

batteries cut loose with a heavy AA fire. At 0045 we secured after another *'busy'* day. Had some difficulty with my passport at Customs inspection as my three month Russian visa had expired while on route during the over four month trip. Every clear day and night while at Nolotovok enemy planes came over but dropped no bombs. Did drop numerous large flares and the Russians concentrated on the flares with apparently 20mm guns. Those flares that they could not reach seemed to remain stationery in the city, some for 15 minutes, but usually for only ten minutes. They were excellent flares, lighting the area very nicely

7 Oct. 1942 - we completed discharging cargo and I left the ship just before it pulled away from the dock at about 1300. Commander Tulley and I took up quarters in the Ford Bodnnon in a flat car. We had canned food with us and was all set for a long train trip to Moscow. Commander Tulley returned to Archanglesk for his baggage and I accompanied the three freight cars on to Moscow, arriving there at about 0530 October 17, 1942 after a most interesting trip, but a most miserable cold journey. Had many interesting conversations with troops en route to the front, with wounded troops and hospital attendants on a hospital train and with troops on a troop train returning to base for refitting from the Stalingrad front. In all cases the morale of the Russian personnel was very high and they all seemed eager to continue the fight until the Axis powers are completely destroyed. Those from the front were most enthusiastic about the performance of the American made Jeeps. Most of them asked:
 'When will American & English forces open the second front?'

The troops en route to the front were young, fresh and well-equipped while the ones from the Stalingrad front were tired and worn, and their clothes and shoes almost completely worn out. All cases, however, the food served them was entirely adequate and none appeared to be in the least undernourished. A number of women accompanied the troops as nurses, chauffeurs and cooks."

This ends the formerly **CONFIDENTIAL** US Navy report dated 23 November 1942 on the voyage of ***Convoy PQ.18***.

CHAPTER 20

Flying Combat with the *Luftwaffe III*

More from Member Baron GEORG von ZIRK.

It was in late spring 1943, during my flight training at Navigator Bombardier School at Thorn, Poland. We were on a bomb training mission, flying the Heinkel bomber. This was for us trainees, the *'real thing'* compared with FW 156 we had to fly in the early stages of our training. This plane, the FW 156 with its 3 men crew, was originally intended as a medium bomber. It was covered with fabric and was called, by its crews, *LEUKOPLAST-BOMBER*, or *'Band-Aid Bomber'*.

So here we were on this flight - three trainees were taking turns in the bomb runs. We were dropping three cement bombs each, on a wooden target 15,000 feet below. Only one trainee at a time was with the pilot and instructor in the cockpit. The rest was in the rear section.

I had already completed my bomb run and had retired to the rear. I was lying on a cushion on the floor, where the rear gunner station was. It was also the hatch through which the crew was boarding the plane. The hatch was opening up to the inside. The roar of the engines had made me drowsy and I was taking a nap. Suddenly the plane dropped in an air pocket. The hatch unlocked itself, lifted up and I fell to my waist outside.

I just managed to spread my arms and hold on to the fuselage. The slipstream was sucking me outside and I was fighting for my life. Two of my comrades came quickly to my aid and pulled me back in. I had no parachute on at the time.

Later in spring of 1944, I was flying combat with **II. Group** (2nd Group) of **KG 55** (Kampfgeschwader *GREIF*). Grief means *'Griffin'*. It was our coat of arms, painted on the fuselages of our bombers. The Russians had launched a large spring offensive in the Ukraine. Each night we were making heavy bombing raids on their rail stations, filled with fuel and ammunition supplies, on the way to the front.

What a fireworks this was, when the rail cars were blowing up. Huge explosions were reaching up to 500 meters. Homebound already from 100 kilometers we could still see the explosions.

When there was no flying weather (We called it *QBI*), the Squadron issued Schnapps and brandy to us. Often we sweetened the Schnapps with honey. This brew we called *'Bärenfang'* or *'Bear Catcher'*. The whole squadron was getting drunk. Sometimes even the officers joined us.

Our crew had the nickname *PICHELSTEINER*. Picheln was an old German expression for drinking.

Anyhow, here we were at it again. Everybody was living it up, because tomorrow we might not come back from a mission, like so many other crews. One of our soldier songs said:
'Heute rot und Morgen tot.'

It means:
'Today Red and tomorrow dead'.

We were assigned about 15 men to a room in our barracks. With the doors open, singing and laughter was coming from everywhere. Some guys had painted on mustaches (growing one was against regulations). Hans, our radioman, had already discarded his shirt and was racing with others on bicycles, down the corridor of the barracks. At the end were swinging doors - but this did not stop them.

We spent almost the whole night drinking - then at 4:30 AM was wake-up call. We were to fly a supply to the Fortress Kovel, which was besieged by the Russians.

With hangovers and not quite sober yet, we collected our flight gear. Our gunner still had make-up on his face and we removed it with frozen snow on our way to the field.

We fired up our engines and the roar of the 60 engines was deafening. One by one we taxied to the runway. There we lined up and each 90 seconds, were given the signal for take off by the Officer in Charge. He stood for each of us at attention and saluted us as we were taking off. This was custom with the bombers.

I was setting course to the airfield at Baranowitsche, located west of Minsk in Bielorussia. There we were loaded with the supply bombs. On the way to Kovel, we met up with a single FW fighter, flying by at a distance. After one-hour flight, Kovel was in our sight. As we got near to the target, we saw puffs of smoke appear below. The Russians were shooting at us with medium Flak.

We made a steep left turn and from 2,000 meters were diving steeply into the cauldron. At about 100 meters we leveled off.

I had my hands full, getting ready for the drop and giving our pilot commands for direction. We were flying at high speed over the small town. Halfway down, I pulled the bomb release. I saw 7 parachutes open up and float down. The eighth did not.

I saw the 250 kg (500 pound) container hit in an orchard and bounce off the ground and slam into a house, which disappeared in a cloud of dust. Several weeks later, I read an article in a military paper where an SS General, Commander of the Fortress Kovel, was describing his experience with *'that damn supply bomb'* which hit the back room of his headquarters

We left Kovel flying low and following railroad tracks. Suddenly we saw on it, a Russian tank. Soldiers were cowering behind it. They were surprised as we were, and no shots were fired.

Soon we reached the German lines. We saw our soldiers in white camouflage suits, wildly waving at us. This was the only time we had such a close look at the war on the ground.

We landed at Baranowitsche and after refueling and reloading, we took off for our second mission. We were flying three bombers in formation.

Everything was routine until half hour into the flight. Suddenly, our left engine began vibrating violently. Seconds later there was an explosion, and flames shot out from the engine. We were trailing black smoke behind us.

Oberleutnant Werner Frick, the pilot, shut off the engine and feathered the prop. The flight engineer shut off the fuel. We slowed down and the other planes pulled away from us. We went into a steep dive and managed to blow out the fire.

In the meantime, I had pulled the bomb emergency release and dropped the supply bombs into a forest. But we were still loosing altitude fast. Then I realized that we had still the huge wooden box under the fuselage. It had to be released electrically. I pushed a button and the box was released. I saw it float down on the parachute. It hit rail tracks and burst open. People were coming running from the nearby station and were helping themselves to the chocolate, which was in the box. The other containers were later recovered from the forest and brought back to the airfield.

We flew back to Baranowitsche on one engine and made a good wheels down landing. During the war we had to come home and land on one engine four times!

The mechanics found out that a broken oil line had caused the engine to freeze up and explode. It had to be replaced and took two days. Although our engines were routinely replaced every 50 hours, sometimes they didn't last that long.

We got time off and were driven to town where we got some beer. We were glad that we had made it back in one piece. Although we had to scrap the mission, we had a saying:
   "Who knows what it was good for?"

After returning to our home base, we heard bad news. One of the crewmembers with our flight had been killed over the target by enemy fire. The night before, we had celebrated with him. That's how it was;
   'HEUTE ROT UND MORGEN TOT!'

Once we had to tow out a *LASTENSEGLER* (transport glider) from the airfield Demblin/Poland. It was a *GOTHA 242* weighing 7143 pounds. She could carry 19 soldiers with equipment. Frick, our pilot, had previous experience in towing gliders. He had been with a Transport-Geschwader where he was towing *GIGANTEN (Me 321)*.

Three Heinkel 111 were needed to get this monster into the air. Demblin airfield was quite short, even for normal takeoffs but with a glider in tow, it became critical. We were barreling down the runway. As we were approaching the fence at the end of the runway and were still not airborne, we realized that we would not make it.

But there was no turning back now. Frick pulled up in the last minute and we jumped the fence. The plane settled back to the ground again and we kept on rolling over plowed fields. Finally at 185 km we lifted off, barely hanging on. In front loomed another obstacle - a five story apartment complex! Oberleutnant Frick was bearing down on it, gaining speed. In the last moment he pulled up and we jumped over it. It lifted us off the seats. We had made it but barely. We never wanted to tow a glider again!

In April 1944 we were attacking the rail yard at Falstoff, south of Kiev. It was a beautiful starry night. From far we could see already the heavy flak over the target. And then we heard over our intercom:
   "To everybody. We are hit and have to bail out!!"

We felt sorry for the poor devils who had to jump from 15,000 feet. Even if they managed to bail out and land safely, they were doomed. The Russians were not taking German bomber crews prisoner. They were shooting them.

Later we found out that it was a crew from the 3rd Squadron on their first mission. Two months later, one of the five got back to us. Ukrainian partizans, who were fighting the Communists, had rescued him. The Fähnrich (cadet) had broken both his legs as bailing out, he hit the stabilizer. They drove him back 250 miles to the German lines in a horse buggy.

When we arrived over the target, the rail yard was burning already from end to end. Crews ahead of us had done their work. The flak was plastering us with heavy salvos. The tracers of the medium flak looked like a string of pearls reaching at us. I put my bombs on the target and saw several large explosions.

On the way back, trouble was waiting for us too. About 100 km from our frontline, we lost an engine. We feathered the prop and the flight engineer and I were giving the pilot assistance, holding opposite rudder against the heavy pressure from the running engine. After two hours, we landed safely at our field at Biakystok. It was already dawning, but I was not done yet. I was driven to the briefing room where I had to make my report about the mission.

Then we were driven to the mess hall and had something to eat. Finally I could go to bed, but I could not fall asleep. For two hours, my ears were still ringing from the engine noise. I was also thinking about the unfortunate crew which had been shot down. We had been lucky that night and had beaten the odds - but for how long? The war was still to last for over one year.

CHAPTER 21

The P-40 Aircraft

From Member PEN HARMS

The P-40 aircraft was if not the only, at least the best game in town for the Allies at the start of World War II. They can be likened to the American "Unique 39" single stack destroyers of the USN – well armed, fast and capable, holding the line until other designs could be built and delivered. They were colloquially names *'HAWKS'* but were also called such variants as *MOHAWK* (Hawk 81A), *WARHAWK, TOMAHAWK* and *KITTYHAWK* (followed by various Mk numbers) by the British.

So, at the risk of sounding like the *'begats'* in the bible: first came the XP-40, then the production model the Hawk 81A, two hundred of which were ordered by the US Army Air Corps, the first three of which were prototypes and the balance delivered to the 33rd Fighter Squadron in Iceland in June of 1941. Note that there was no P-40A.

Then came the P-40B of which 131 were initially produced, introducing cockpit armor, four wing machine guns and two nose guns. These were called the TOMAHAWK MkIIA by the British and Hawk 81A2 by the Americans. The British contingent went to the Middle East. One hundred of these were diverted to the AVG (American Volunteer Group otherwise known as the Flying Tigers) in China.

The P-40C (or Hawk 81A-3) had self-sealing fuel tanks. Only 193 were produced for American use, the remainder going to Britain and the USSR. It was found to be the slowest of the plane's versions to date, and was used primarily in ground attacks.

Then came the P-40D (Hawk 87A-2) with a major nose redesign with the radiator moved forward. Provision was made in this model for carrying a single 500 lb. bomb or a drop tank under the fuselage. Only 23 of these variants were produced for the U.S.

The P-40-E (Hawk 81A-3) was the first WARHAWK P-40 series to go into production after Pearl Harbor. The WARHAWK designation was the American name for the plane, the British preferred KITTY HAWK – this model the Mk1A. These planes were used by the RAF, Royal Australian Air Force, Royal New Zealand Air Force and Royal Canadian Air Force.

Another modification was the P-40F, designed to use the more powerful Merlin engine (the previous models used Allison). These craft featured a lengthened fuselage by 20 inches and maximum weight of 9,870 pounds. Top speed however, dropped to 365 mph.

At the same time the P-40F variants were being produced, the P-40K models were also in production, with a speed increase to 366 mph and a more powerful Allison engine. It had a slight edge over the Me 109 and the Mitsubishi A6M.

More power was provided for the P-40M. These were called the KITTYHAWK Mk III by the Royal Air Force.

Only a few of the P-40G models were built, and retained by the USAAF. The P-40J was supposed to have turbocharged Allison engines, but used the Merlin instead. The P-40L built in 1943 for the USAAF also used the Merlin engine.

The P-40N reverted to the Allison power plant, and had wing racks to carry two additional 500 lb bombs. Just over 200 finally arrived with this modification for bombing attacks. The British version, some 500 planes, were known as the KITTYHAWK MkIV. In 1944 there were additional experimental models including the P-40Q with Allison engines and the radiators moved to the wings.

The total production of these planes in all variants for the period totaled 16,802 which included 4,787 contracted by Great Britain.

The WARHAWKS (all inclusive P-40) served in almost all fronts of World War Two and provided little publicized support as the USAAF fighter defense in the Panama Canal 1941 – 1943.

Both Britain and France had initially contracted for these planes before the USA entered the war, the first British contingent being used at first for training since they lacked armament protection. The French shipment was diverted when the government fell.

The War Department's first order for the P-40, issued in 1939, was valued at $12,872,898 and consisted of 524 planes. At the time it was the largest contract issued for combat planes since World War I. Today that entire contract might buy one third of just one HARRIER jet fighter. The first production models came off the line in spring of 1940 and approximately 200 were delivered by September. One hundred forty were turned over to the British, although originally ordered by the French. These planes were referred to by the British as TOMAHAWK MkI and were assigned to training units due to lack of armor and insufficient armament.

The second version, the P-40B (WARHAWK) appeared in 1941 carrying cockpit armor, two additional machine guns and self-sealing fuel tanks. The first of the aircraft were assigned in Britain to the 2, 13, 26, 94, 112, 171, 150, 268, 400, 403 and 414 Squadrons, being a shipment originally intended for France and were designated as TOMAHAWKs. The fully armed versions were also shipped as HA (Hawk-A) and HB (Hawk-B) to the U.K. and West Africa, operating in the Middle East. TOMAHAWKs were also supplied to South Africa, Turkey and the USSR.

The planes operating in the Middle East went into action in June 1941 and the Number 3 Squadron of the RAAF used P-40's in their strafing runs on Rommel's troops and supply lines. The Russian contingent initially was 146 of the IIB model, shipped from the reserve forces in the U.K., with 49 additional planes coming directly from the USA. These craft went into action in October 1941 defending Moscow and Leningrad.

It was this version assigned to the RAF Desert Air Force 112 Squadron who painted shark mouths on the fuselages. This design appeared in the 112 Squadron in September 1941. The exact date is unknown, but it is believed that it was originally painted as a personal insignia then copied by the entire squadron.

One hundred, originally assigned for Britain, were diverted to China, for use by the AVG. There were sixty-two P-40B and eleven P-40C fighters there when Pearl Harbor was attacked on December 7th, 1941.

The Aleutian area also had the P-40, and the 343rd Fighter Group, 11th Fighter Squadron in the Aleutians was commanded by Lt. Col. John Chenault. The shark mouth, now enhanced with the entire animal's head, was used in tribute to his father. It should also be noted that in 1942, this group carried the national insignia on their P-40E fighters, which was the white star only, without a surround. This was a rare variation, used only in the Pacific in 1942. These planes were specially winterized for operations in the far north.

The plane was criticized by some, because of some of its performance characteristics, particularly at high altitude. However, as the AVG numbers indicate, the pilots were able to use both the strengths and the shortcomings to their advantage. In fact, the RAAF pilots later adopted the tactics developed by the AVG. Whether this was by word of mouth, pilot-to-pilot or (less likely) by official report, in unknown.

The P-40E had some of these problems solved, and all 2,320 of them carried heavier armament. They were the first model to see service with the USAAF in Europe, primarily used in the Mediterranean. The P-40F was further improved with a Rolls-Royce Merlin engine, build by agreement in the USA by Packard Company. Many of these engines were also assigned to the later and more effective P-51 MUSTANG.

The D through M variants of the P-40 were known as the WARHAWK and in Britain, the KITTYHAWK. The N through Q variants were known only as WARHAWKS and the N variant were supplied to Britain for use in the Mediterranean and middle east, and to the South Pacific for use by the Royal New Zealand Air force.

With this long production period (1939 through 1944) the Curtiss P-40 models were distinguished by their pilots, who used both the strengths and the shortcomings of these planes to their advantage. In this regard, the story of the aircraft cannot be told without telling something of those who flew them.

Mention has to be made of the 112 Squadron, RAF and their use of the shark mouth. But the most famous group to use this trademark was the AVG – the Flying Tigers. Their private insignias included (literally) a flying tiger and the "hell's angel" – this one used by R. T. Smith, one of the original AVG members.

Under the command of General Claire Chenault, these men took their limited number of aircraft; only 90 of the original planes reached Kyedaw, and carrying the Chinese blue and white insignia and with their American pilots, began operating out of Kumming and Mingaladon in December 1941. The primary purpose STATED for the AVG at that time was the protection of the Burma Road and areas on the Chinese-Burmese border. These P-40B fighters along with some thirty P-40E aircraft accounted for 286 AVG victories against Japanese aircraft. These pilots developed tactics wherein the P-40's superior speed and more durable construction was able to counter the superior climb rate and maneuverability of the Japanese fighters. In March 1942, only about twenty of the original P-40 fighters were airworthy; the damaged planes were cannibalized to keep the remaining ones flying. Only 30 additional planes were ferried to the AVG in early 1942.

The abilities of these pilots, using their personal flying skills, common sense and having a loyalty to their commander, flew with a vengeance; and the scores attest to their dedication. After the USA entered the war, the AVG were ignominiously told to either 'sign up' for the USAAF or go home and be drafted, probably to end up in a trench somewhere in Europe. Their exploits, hazardous and having virtually no backup in materials and the only spare parts available coming from their comrade's aircraft which were no longer serviceable, deserved better. Hollywood, according to one of the original Tigers, got their name out before the public but the story as shown on the screen was fabrication (that wasn't the exact word he used, but you get the message). In fact his comment was that John Wayne's acting was fine, but the picture as a story was total BS. Too bad it took fifty years for them to be recognized!

CHAPTER 22

Luftwaffe's 'Throw Away' Fighter
From Member TIM KUTTA

At the beginning of 1943, the Luftwaffe's ability to conduct heavy bombing raids against enemy targets was severely limited. Losses of aircraft and crews during the air campaigns over England, Russia, North Africa and Italy had reduced the German bomber force to a shell of its once greatness. The bomber forces still had a great many medium bombers but heavy losses, coupled with the growing obsolescence of many of the bombers had reduced the effectiveness of the force. In addition, the growing effectiveness of Allied fighter and antiaircraft defenses was making accurate bombing more and more difficult. While the bomber force was still capable of conducting raids, their ability to hit and destroy targets was limited. In an effort to reverse the effects of obsolete aircraft and young crews, the Luftwaffe put out a specification for a new type of bomber that could be used to destroy crucial enemy targets with pinpoint accuracy.

A conventional bomber would not fit the bill and German aircraft manufacturers were tasked with finding a new way to get the bomber through to its target. The challenge was well met and within a few weeks, several unique and unusual designs were submitted to fill the specification. However of all the proposals, only two, the *MISTEL* and Messerschmitt *Me-328* (previous page) appeared as viable options.

The *MISTEL* was a combination fighter/bomber. This combination consisted of a manned fighter mounted atop a specially modified bomber loaded with explosives (photo below). The fighter pilot flew both aircraft and when he arrived over the target, he dove the combination aircraft at the target, separated from the bomber by way of explosive bolts and then flew back to his base. The bomber slammed into the target at great speed, demolishing both in a great blast.

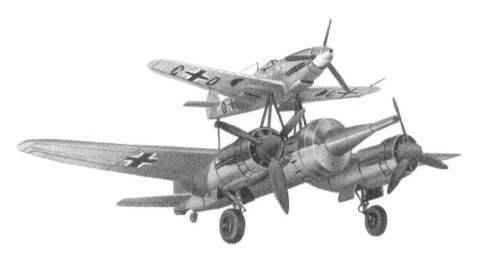

Another design, the Messerschmitt *Me-328*, reversed the process. The fighter was carried atop the bomber much as the *MISTEL* but both aircraft were manned. Near the target, the Messerschmitt *Me-328* would detach and fly on to the target. Once over the target, the pilot would point his fighter at the target, much as the *MISTEL*, and then bail out. The target and fighter would be destroyed in the explosion. The pilot of course, had to walk home but that did not seem a drawback. The Luftwaffe decided to develop both projects simultaneously.

The Messerschmitt *Me-328* was originally conceived as a *Project 1079* in July 1941 as a small fighter that could be carried or towed behind a German bomber. This would allow the bomber to have immediate fighter protection at the exact location it was attacked by the enemy. The fighter would draw fuel from the bomber while it was being towed, thus when it was released its tanks would be full and it would be able to stay in the target area longer than a normal fighter. In order to make it light enough to tow and not to tax the already overburdened German metal industry, the engineers at Messerschmitt planned to construct the fighter out of lightweight, non-strategic materials such as wood. Since the *'Parasite Fighter'* as the aircraft was often called, had a good likelihood of not returning, the engineers wanted to use the cheapest, most efficient source of power they could find. Fortunately, the *Argus As 014* Pulse Jet Engine was available.

The Pulse Jet Engine had been developed by Dr. Paul Schmidt in the early 1920s. The engine was a long tube which allowed air in through a movable shutters, saturated the air with fuel as it flowed through the tube and then, when the shutters closed, the fuel rich air was ignited and the force of the explosion was directed out the back of the tube causing thrust. This process was repeated 50 to 250 times a second and resulted in an engine that produced 660 lbs. of thrust and could propel an aircraft to speeds of 350-400 mph. In addition to the speed, the engine was quite simple to build and maintain, and could burn almost any type of fuel. The only problem with the engine was that it had to have an air supply moving through the tube in order to work. In short, there was no way to run the engine while the aircraft was standing still. However, since the aircraft would be launched in flight, there would already be a suitable supply of air for the engine and the designers did not see this as a problem.

By March 1942, design of the aircraft had progressed sufficiently for the Messerschmitt engineers to submit a proposal to the Air Ministry. The proposal included provisions for six different versions. The *Me-328A-1* was the basic fighter equipped with twin pulse jet engines, one mounted under each wing. It had a 21 ft. wingspan and was 22 ft. 5 in. long. The aircraft was armed with two powerful 20mm *MG 151* cannons. Fully loaded it weighed 4,840 lbs. and had a top speed of 470 mph.

The *Me-328A-2* was the next version and it had four engines, two under each wing. It had a 27 ft. 10 3/4 in. wingspan and was 28 ft. 3 3/4 in. long. The added power of the engines allowed this version to carry a much heavier armament. The aircraft carried two 30mm *MK 103* cannons and two 20mm *MG 151* cannons. It weighed 8,360 lbs. and had a top speed of 570 mph. The next version, the *Me-328A-3* was the basic twin-engine fighter with provisions for air to air refueling. This would allow the fighter to protect the bomber and then once both aircraft had left the target area, the fighter could refuel in the air from the bomber. This would save both the pilot of the fighter and the fighter itself.

The next three versions were fighter-bombers, which featured strengthened fuselages to accommodate the bomb loads. The first of these versions, the *Me-328B-1* was a twin-engine fighter-bomber, similar to the *Me-328A-1*. It could carry 2,205 lbs. of bombs on external racks under the fuselage. It weighed 5,940 lbs. fully loaded and top speed of 423 mph.

The *Me-328B-2* was a four-engine fighter-bomber, similar to the *Me-328A-2*, which could carry a 2,205 pound bomb load on external racks. The *Me-328B-1* weighed 10,405 lbs. and had a top speed of 370 mph. The final version, the *Me-328B-3*, was a twin-engine version equipped to carry the *SD 1400 'Fritz-X'* guided bombs. This involved mounting a joystick and radio guidance equipment in the aircraft but the added weight was insignificant and did not affect the performance of the aircraft.

The Air Ministry was not particularly impressed with the project. At the time it was presented, the Luftwaffe was still a powerful force and holding its own against the enemy air forces. However, when the tide of battle swung against the Germans and they were forced on the strategic defensive, the Luftwaffe began a search for new aircraft. The project was revived to meet the new specification for a new type of long range bomber, which could deliver pinpoint strikes against important enemy targets. There was no need for a fighter version and the *Me-328A* version was canceled. The Air Ministry wanted a disposal bomber that could be carried to the target, launched and then pointed at the target before the pilot bailed out. Just short of a suicide mission, but it offered several advantages. The pilot of the *Me-328B* would only need rudimentary flight instruction. He would not need to know how to take off, land or navigate.

There would be no need to teach him aerial gunnery or how to drop bombs. He would be released close to the target and all he would have to do is point the nose of his bomber at the enemy and bail out. The possibilities appealed to the Air Ministry. Messerschmitt was given permission to build three prototype airframes for tests in March 1943.

Prototype construction began almost immediately. The wooden wings were made in the Messerschmitt plant, while the steel skinned fuselages were produced in **DFS** glider manufacturers' workshops. In order to simply production, a standard **Me-109** tail plane was attached to the fuselage. This speeded production AND saved money, as the tail planes were already in mass production.

Once the prototypes were constructed, the engineers spent a great deal of time getting the aircraft ready for flight. The pulse jet engines were long and bulky and that made attachment difficult. Initially, the engineers thought the wings might not support the engines and tried to attach the engines to brackets on the rear of the fuselage. Thus, the hot exhaust would be vented back underneath and away from the tail. This however, proved unworkable as the weight of the engines made the fuselage very heavy in the rear and that affected the flight characteristics. The engineers were forced to move the engines out to the wings. The engines were a bit heavy for the wings but a bit of strengthening in the wing roots solved the problems. The wings proved quite capable of supporting two or four pulse jet engines.

The initial mockup proved very impressive and Messerschmitt was given authority to build seven additional prototypes to be used for launch and flight trials. The first prototype was ready for tests in the winter of 1943. These were carried out at Linz, where the **Me-328 V1** was attached to two steel triangles mounted on the wing roots of a **Dornier-217E**. These triangles served as attachment point between the **Dornier** and the **Me-328**. The planes separated when the pilot detonated explosive bolts which held the Messerschmitt to the steel triangles. A small flexible steel rod was also attached between the tail of the **Me-328** and the fuselage of the **Dornier**. This kept the tail of the Me from dipping and crashing into the fuselage of the Dornier on separation.

Dornier DO-217

The first tests were unpowered, designed to test the basic airworthiness of the airframe. Several tests were conducted with the aircraft released from altitudes of 9,000 to 18,000 ft. While the aircraft was difficult to handle in the air, the pilot could maintain sufficient control and the testing proceeded to powered flight.

The *Me-328* was equipped with two *Argus As 014* pulsejets AND towed to 9,840 ft by the *Do-217E*. Once at altitude the engines were started and the *Me-328* detached from its *'mother ship'* and flew under its own power. It was the first of many test flights. The flights soon revealed problems with the engines. They delivered the promised power but vibrated during operation. The engine vibrations caused the wings to flutter and the fuselage to shake. On several occasions the vibrations became so severe that the pilot jettisoned both engines.

In addition, two prototypes crashed during the test phase, probably as a result of engine vibration. The engineers tried to fix the problem by moving the engines on the wing. They mounted the engines with the intakes far forward of the wings and then tried them close to the leading edges. The best position was found to be in the center of the wings, which balanced the engines on the wings and gave good airflow to the intakes. The engineers also experimented with where to locate the engines along the wing. They positioned the engines close to the wing root, mid-wing and far out toward the wing tip. The most efficient and strongest position was found to be just outboard of the wing root. This was the strongest and thickest portion of the wing and gave the engines ample support. However, after all the experimentation, the problem was still not fixed. The pulse jet engines simply vibrated too much for the small lightweight wings and airframe of the *Me-328* to absorb.

The engineers even tried to find an alternative engine that would not vibrate as much as the pulsejet. A single engine version with a Junkers *Jumo 004B* turbojet engine mounted in the fuselage was investigated. However, turbojet engines were in short supply and those coming off the production line were allocated to several other more important jet projects. This version never got off the drawing board. By the early spring of 1944 the project had taken up a great deal of time and was in danger of cancellation.

However, Messerschmitt and the Air Ministry decided they could convert the *Me-328* to a manned glider bomb without any difficulty. Without engines, the *Me-328* would be appreciably slower but if it were launched at night it would be difficult for the defenders to detect. Also, removing the fuel and engines would allow the aircraft to carry a greater bomb load. Several *Me-328* prototypes, with their engines removed, were sent to *KG 200* for further development in March 1944.

KG 200 was the Luftwaffe's special operations wing and was tasked with carrying out agent delivery and pick up, attacks on special targets such as bridges, power plants and harbors. Glide trials and evaluation of the weapon were carried out in April by *5/KG 200* which was commanded by Hauptmann Heinrich Lange. Lange was at the time working on **MISTEL** configurations for use against the allied invasion fleet which was expected in the summer of 1944.

The trials established that the *Me-328* could easily be carried aloft aboard the German bombers assigned to the squadron. Tests showed that the *Me-328*, released from an altitude of 10,000 feet could fly toward the target in a shallow dive, which would give the glider a speed of 155 mph. Once over the target, the pilot would increase the angle of the dive to near vertical, release the rear section of the fuselage and bail out. Once in the dive, the glider would reach speeds of 440 mph. Lange planned to put 2,205 lbs. of bombs in the glider and the combined effect of the speed and bomb the load was certain to destroy any target the *Me-328* hit.

A production order for several dozen *Me-328s* was given to Messerschmitt but production delays kept the aircraft out of operations against the D-day invasion force. After the invasion, the swarming Allied night fighters convinced the pilots of *5/KG 200* that neither *MISTEL* configuration nor a bomber carrying the *Me-328* glide bomb was fast enough to penetrate the Allied defenses. The order for the *Me-328s* was canceled before any production aircraft were delivered.

Thus ended one of the Reich's strangest aircraft. The *Me-328* was one of the first piloted aircraft designed around a pulse jet engine. It was envisioned as a parasite fighter, which could be carried to the target area aboard German bombers; fight off enemy fighters until its fuel ran out, allowing the bomber to carry out its vital mission. The ambitious program also called for a fighter bomber version, which could provide the Luftwaffe with a high speed bomber which would also be making a one way trip. But the engineers could never get the pulse jet engines to work correctly and the *Me-328* ended its career as a piloted glider loaded with explosives. It was truly Messerschmitt's disposable aircraft.

CHAPTER 23

The Heinkel HE 177

From Member TIM KUTTA

The Heinkel HE-177 was an extraordinary airplane. It embodied the finest and most advanced German aerodynamic engineering techniques. It was so incredibly advanced for its time and yet it was a total failure. Teething problems, technical difficulties and its propensity to catch fire in the air marked it as one of the most unloved aircraft in the Luftwaffe inventory. Yet at one point in the war, the Heinkel HE-188 represented the only weapon that could change the course of the war on the Eastern Front.

In the late 1930's the Luftwaffe was building and growing by leaps and bounds. New planes, doctrine and tactics were emerging daily. Young, aggressive pilots coupled with a cadre of older officers who had transferred from the infantry and other combat arms were building a young and dynamic organization.

The new Luftwaffe was aided by an emerging and energetic aircraft industry. Dornier, Junkers, Messerschmitt, Focke-Wulf and Heinkel were all producing new and impressive aircraft. In many cases, the Luftwaffe Generals didn't have to request an airplane; the designers in the various firms were always coming forward with new designs and proposals for airplanes that might be needed by the German war machine.

Amid this heady atmosphere, General Walther Weaver, the first Chief of the Luftwaffe General Staff, began to speak of long-range four-engine heavy bombers which could reach the Russian factories in the Ural Mountains. The *'URAL BOMBER'* as the concept became known was probably little more than a dream for the General. After its initial proposal, two firms submitted designs. Both were substandard and the project was shelved.

In 1938, Ernst Heinkel, the head of Heinkel Aircraft, submitted a proposal to build the *'URAL BOMBER'*. His proposal was numbered as the He P.1041. He thought he could build the new bomber and have it operational by 1940. The Luftwaffe was of course, doubtful of the proposal, but since Heinkel was the only manufacturer to try, they gave him the opportunity.

Heinrich Hertel, the Chief of Development for the Heinkel Aircraft Company was told that to satisfy the Luftwaffe, he would have to build a plane capable of carrying 2,000 lbs. of bombs over a range of 4,160 miles. The new bomber had to have a top speed of 335 mph and be able, if necessary, act as a dive bomber. This was a tall order even for the competent designers of Heinkel. However, Hertel had a talented designer working for him named Siegfried Gunter. His genius coupled with Hertel's experience, produced a rather remarkable aircraft. The plane featured four engines were coupled into two nacelles, remote-controlled gun turrets and wing evaporation cooling for the engines. Due to the fact that it incorporated so many new and untried features, the prototypes were frequently modified to overcome problems.

When it finally reached production, the new bomber, which was called the *GREIF* or *GRIFFIN*, had a span of 103 feet 1 inch. It was 66 feet 11 inches long and stood 20 feet 11 inches high. It was powered by four 12-cylinder Daimler-Benz engines which were coupled into two pairs. The coupled engines were called *DB 606*'s. Each was rated at 2,700 hp. These engines gave the production versions a top speed of 317 mph at 19,030 feet. The new bomber was heavily armed with three 7.93mm *MG*

81s machine guns; three 13mm *MG 131s* machine guns; and two 20mm *FF* cannon. The bomber was equipped with two bomb bays which could carry a maximum load of 2,205 lbs. of bombs. The Heinkel HE-177 had a crew of five, maximum take-off weight of 68,343 lbs. and range of 3,417 miles.

Heinkel He-177

Despite its troubled beginning and bad reputation, the Heinkel HE-177 was used extensively in the later part of the war. The total production run amounted to eleven hundred and sixty one bombers. If the teething problems had been worked out earlier, the bomber might well have given the Luftwaffe a powerful weapon to use on both the Eastern and Western Fronts.

CHAPTER 24

My Three Great Escapes from the Communists

From Member Baron GEORG von ZIRK

GEORG von ZIRK was a Luftwaffe Navigator-Bombardier who flew 81 combat missions with 1 and 2 Staffel II Gruppe of KG 55 GREIF (Griffin) & 9 Staffel III Gruppe Zielfinder-Verband KG 4 GENERAL WEVER; IV Fliegerkorps, Luftflotte 6

This was written for Sharkhunters by Baron von ZIRK 1995.

It is fifty years now since the war ended. Fifty years, but we soldiers who, on orders from our government, had to fight it, can never forget. After we came back, we tried to live a normal life. We started out with nothing. We, who were already married, tried to continue where we had left off. I had married in the last months of the war. After the wedding, I went back to the front. The fighting continued.

Now our task was not to bomb the enemy but to supply our troops in many fortress cities, from the air with supplies. We, the crew of *9 Staffel* of *III PATHFINDER Group*, General Wever, flew night missions to Budapest, Breslau and Berlin. In the last few months I flew twelve missions to Budapest, six to Breslau and one to Berlin. We lost many crews. Our Heinkel bomber also received many hits from fighter attack and Flak.

We were sold out!

On 28 April 1945 *ANTON KURFURST* flew its last mission of the war. We had survived the war, but our fate was uncertain. On May 3, our Group Commander, Major Graubner had us assembled. We called him '*Bubi*' because of his young age. In pompous words, he announced:

'Our Führer had just fallen in Berlin, leading our troops against the enemy. This is the end but don't worry, I am going to lead you all home, in one unit.'

The next day, we received orders to destroy our planes! They explained to us that our troops, who covered our retreat, would need the fuel from our planes. We started the engines and pulled in the gears, and dropped our planes on the ground. What a sad sight it was to see our planes lying with bent props.

Two hours later came another order - *'Blow up the planes.'*

With this, our Command had delivered us to the enemy. There had been rumors that they had negotiated with the Russians for surrender. Our Command had sold us out in the last days of the war. Major Graubner had saved his plane and flew with his crew home, right to the very door steps of his house. After the war, I had the chance to meet his pilot and he told me this.

On the 6th of May, we were ordered to get ready to leave our airfield at Königgratz Czechoslovakia. We packed our gear and boarded trucks. What we could not carry, we smashed to pieces. As we were driving that late afternoon through the streets of town, we saw them lined with crowds;
'Vengeance for Lidice!' they shouted.

This was the Czech village which the SS had destroyed in retribution for the assassination of SS Führer Heidrich. As we were driving west, we had to fight it out with the Czech Partisans, who had set up numerous roadblocks. But they were no fighters. A few rounds from our submachine guns had them running.

Overhead we saw an American scout plane.

We were making very slow headway. The highway was clogged with troops of all kind of army units. Often we had to stop and wait for hours until we could move on. Overhead we saw an American scout plane but no Russians who were one day behind us.

On the 10th of May we arrived in the small town of Pisek, at the River Motlava. We heard rumors that we were going to surrender to the Americans who were already here, but they didn't let us cross to the other side.

We were waiting and wondering what was going to happen. An American jeep drove up with some officers. Soon we received orders to clean up the highway; move our vehicles and gear out of the way because American troops were supposed to pass through.

We were being sold to the Russians; Our wounded and women were sold too!

The Americans came back to inspect. Then we were told that we also had to pick up the straw scattered on the ground. It became clear to us that the Americans were just stalling us so the Russians could catch up with us. We saw busses with wounded German soldiers and their nurses sent back, who had already crossed here days before.

I disassembled my *MP40* and my *08* (Luger) and scattered the pieces on a field. I buried my medals, badges and Wehrpass (German Army Passport), which the Squadron had given us back in the last days. Why? So *'Ivan'* would know exactly that we were from KG 4 which in 1944 had bombed their rail stations into the ground? We knew now that the Americans would turn us over to the Russians.

They arrived in the afternoon. I saw one Russian soldier coming down the road. I never forget this sight. He was dressed in a shabby drab uniform, but was armed with a submachinegun. They called it *'PEPESHKA'*.

The first thing he asked us:
 'Germanski! dawa! UHR! UHR!'
  ('Germans! Quick! Watch! Watch!')

He wanted out watches first, not our guns. He already had about ten watches strapped on each arm. Later we saw others throwing watches away because they had stopped.
 'UHR Kaputt!'

They didn't know that they had to be wound up.

EDITOR NOTE – That famous photograph of the Russian soldier of Zhukov's Red Army who was high atop the German Reichstag with the Soviet Union Flag had to be reshot for propaganda purposes. The reason – the soldier with the flag had both arms covered with wrist watches stolen from German prisoners. They reshot the photograph after he had removed all the watches.

The Russians assembled all Germans - soldiers and civilian refugees in a nearby forest. We were about 11,000 troops and many German civilian refugees.

They surrounded us with cannons and machine guns. Next day they sent groups of their soldiers to talk to us.
 '*Skoro damoi!*'

They were saying,
 '*In two weeks you will all be going home.*

I knew it was a lie, thanks to my education by my uncle, as a boy. He was in WW I a Colonel of the Czarist Army. I knew the Russian mentality. I knew we would be sent into captivity for years to come. I made my decision to escape as soon as I got a chance.

I was preparing myself. I walked around among the civilians, who had already thrown most of their stuff away - mainly clothing. I picked up a pair of civilian pants and hid them in my knapsack. I had also kept my summer flight jacket, from which I cut off the Luftwaffe Eagle. I had kept a can of meat and my canteen, two watches and a compass. Most important - I had an American map of whole Europe printed on silk which I had recovered from a downed American flier.

It was Russian soldier's right to rape all the German women and girls. Ehrenberg told them so.

We were kept here for three days. I had hitched up with a German refugee girl. She was afraid of the Russians. She knew what they would do to her. The Russians had raped German women and girls as soon as they reached German land. This was their reward, promised to them by Stalin and Elia Ehrenburg, the Russian version of Josef Goebbels.

In the evening of the third day, we had to assemble and were marched off to the East. We were on our way to Russia. The women had to stay behind - at the mercy of the Russians.

After marching for several hours, around midnight we reached a small town. The Russians had not given us any food. Some soldiers rushed to a fountain for water but our officers did not let us drink. There was no order given to drink! Can you believe that? Here we were, all in Russian captivity and our officers were still giving us orders. The Russians found it ridiculous and gave us permission to drink.

We moved on. The second stop we had around three O'Clock in the morning. We set down along the side of the highway. On one side was a forest. This looked good to me and I made my decision to escape.

I had a glimpse of Unteroffizier Heinmann, my Flight Engineer. He was sitting a few feet away from me. Oberleutnant Frick, my pilot was somewhere up front of the column together with the other officers. The others of our crew, Radioman Feldwebel Will and Gunner, Unteroffizier Schulz, we had lost already days ago after we had left Königgratz.

But I could not take them with me. My escape plan was based on my knowledge of the Russian language, in which I was fluent. So everybody was on his own and fate would decide who would survive. Heinemann and Schulz died later in Russian camps. Frick returned after four years in captivity. He and I are now the only survivors of the crew of our Heinkel HE 111 bomber named *ANTON KURFURST*.

Every fifteen meters were guards with submachine guns. As the nearest to me looked the other way, I was on my feet and running at full speed into the forest. The dice were cast. I was waiting for shots to ring out, but nothing happened. My escape had not been noticed.

I ran about 200 meters into the woods and stopped. As I was catching my breath, I heard my comrades singing as they marched off into captivity. They sang an old soldier song,
   'In the homeland we will see each other again.'

I had to go back to the highway to pick up my knapsack. I had dropped it after I had run a few yards. It was still there and I went back into the forest. I had to hurry because it was dawning already. I took off my uniform and changed into the civilian pants and the flight jacket. Then I crawled under bushes and covered myself with my blanket. I camouflaged it from above with twigs. When it was done, it was daylight already. I had to wait now until it got dark once again.

It was quiet, almost eerie. It was like the world had come to a standstill. Only once in a while I heard the sound of a pheasant or the bark of a fox. My mind was working on my escape plan. My plan was to get through to the American lines, about 90 miles away. I would march only at night, hiding during daylight. I would use no roads. I would go on a SW course across forests, fields and rivers, avoiding any settlements as much as possible. I had to avoid the Russian soldiers, definitely Czech partisans and also civilians.

As it got dark, I took off and marched all night. In the morning I still wasn't out of the forest. I hid under the brush, hoping that I would not encounter any partisans.

At dusk, I took off again and marched all night long, using my Luftwaffe compass for direction. I arrived at a forest path and followed it. Suddenly I heard hoofbeats! I left the path and jumped into the bushes. I was making noises like a deer, crashing through the brush. When I reached an open field, I stopped for a moment. Nobody was coming after me. What had I encountered out here?

I felt pain in my shin. I must have hurt it when I jumped into the bushes. I moved on and again had to go through wooded area. It was very dark and sometimes I had to feel my way forward. Suddenly I reached a steep slope. I had to sit down and slide forward on my rear. I couldn't see nothing. Finally I arrived at the bottom and I was out of the woods.

I had arrived at a river. It was about 20 meters wide and had a swift current. I didn't know if it was deep. I decided to cross to the other side and waded into the water. After a few steps, it reached to my knees and the current was sweeping me off my feet. I did not dare go on with my heavy gear, and I turned back.

I followed the riverbank until I saw some houses in the distance. It was getting light and I had to look for a hiding place. I found it in a large straw stack about 400 meters from the village. I climbed to the top and hid in the straw. I was cold from my wet shoes and pants. When the sun came out, it got a little better.

When the Russian soldiers were mingling among us, I overheard them saying that they would pull back and the Americans would take over this territory. So once in a while, I was sticking out my head and looking around. In the distance I could hear some trucks driving, and I speculated that there must be a highway. I was wondering if it were the Americans, but I could not distinguish anything.

As I stuck my head out late in the afternoon, a Czech farmer spotted me. He must have observed me before, because it looked like he was waiting.

'Kamerad SS, come on out!' he shouted.

So this was the moment of truth for which I had prepared myself mentally. I knew that sooner or later, I would have to face my enemies. But how would I make out? There was no time to think. Calmly I came out and spoke to the Czech in Russian. I said to him that I was escaping from the Germans. I pretended that I didn't know the war was over.

It didn't take long and about 50 armed men were surrounding me. Everybody was asking questions, and I had to have the right answers. I had to empty my pockets. The Luftwaffe compass, Astro watch and map did not make them suspicious. They were just farmers. After I had answered all their questions in fluent Russian, they were satisfied. They gave me back my gear and the farmer who had found me, took me to his house. There I got something to eat. This was the first real food in a week.

In the afternoon I was told that I should walk to the next town and report to the Militia. I thanked the farmer and left. I was really glad to be on the road again and this time right in the open. As a *'Russian'* I had the right. I had passed the first test.

As I was leaving the village, I heard shouting behind me. The farmer gave me an escort to show me the way. Apparently they wanted to make sure I got there. This complicated things for me. I had not intended to report at the Militia post. Besides, I remembered that I still carried my *FRONTFLUGAUSWEIS* (my Luftwaffe identification) with me. The farmers had missed it in my hip pocket. I had figured that if I could not talk my way out, as a member of the Luftwaffe I had a better chance to survive than being taken for SS. Those they killed on the spot.

We were walking along the riverbank. Pretending that I had to relieve myself, I went down to the water where I slipped my whole wallet, with ID, photos and all, into the water. Being all *'Russian'* was the only to go. When we arrived at the Militia post, the Czech guard greeted me in German:
"You German swine, now we got you!"

When I told him that I was Russian, he was quite startled. I was led inside and faced several partisans. Now they called themselves a Militia. They began interrogating me. Who was I? Where did I come from? I stuck with my original story.

My pockets were emptied and again the usual contents did not make them overly suspicious - but they *'confiscated'* everything except a bandage. In it I had hidden my private watch. They had not noticed and I could keep it.

Two hours later, their Commander walked in. He wore a civilian jacket, military breeches and riding boots. From his pocket showed a Luger. Without saying a word, he walked around me, looked me over from head to toe. I was standing in the middle of the room and everybody was watching me. My nerves were calm, as I was on a combat mission.

"So you claim to be from Lwow."
He began his interrogation. (Lwow was a city in eastern Poland. I knew it vaguely from a time when I passed through twice).

The interrogation continued;
"Tell me the name of the main street,"

he continued;
"Describe me the rail station; how many tracks has it? What is the name of the main street?"

and so on and so on.

I thought he probably never was there himself. I answered his questions at random, but in detail. After twenty minutes of interrogation, he slapped me on the shoulder. Turning around, he told his men that I was okay.

They put me in a room and I went to sleep on the bunk bed. When I woke up the next morning, I saw that a German Luftwaffe Sergeant was with me in the room. He was still in uniform. I ignored him, for fear that the Czechs might have set me a trap. He and I had the same Luftwaffe sweaters on!

Two guards picked us up later and escorted us to a military barracks. After waiting a while, a Russian showed up. After talking to me, he told me to report at Budweis at the Russian Headquarters. I could go. I was quite relieved when I walked past the sentry. When I was out of sight, I got rid of my sweater and the Luftwaffe knapsack.

I came to a village full of Hungarian soldiers. They had fought on our side, but the Russians let them go home. I got a small piece of bread from them. At dark, I moved on and walked all night. I got into a lake region and it took me some time until I found my way out of there. I reached a village. The houses were all dark but one. I heard voices from inside. Since I was hungry and thirsty, I decided to knock.

The voices stopped and when I knocked again, the door sprang open. I saw two rifles and then two Militiamen rushing outside. They wanted to know who I was and why I was out after curfew hours. I told my old story and that I was just looking for food.

They told me that they didn't have any for me. In the ensuing conversation, I found out that there was a Russian bakery in the next village. Now I insisted that I wanted to go there right away. I told them they had no right to hold a Russian. They let me go but two guys followed me for a while. After I was out of sight, I resumed my course.

When it got light, I hid in a grain field. Since it was not very tall, I had to look for a spot which would cover me. The sun was burning on me all day. It was agony. I had some water in my canteen, but no food.

After dark, I moved on and walked all night. At dawn, I hid in a grain field again because there was no other place to hide. Again I lay all day in the hot sun. Finally it was getting dark. I was just about to get to my feet when I heard voices. They were getting close. My first impulse was to run, but I stayed put. Now they were on top of me. I was laying face down, and I saw a boot stepping beside my head. They walked past without noticing me. I waited until it was all quiet. I never knew who they were, but probably some partisans.

I moved on. At dawn I was approaching a village and I hid in a haystack. Later it began raining and rained all day. In the late afternoon, wet and cold, I could not stand it any longer in my hideout. I had to get out, no matter what happened.

When I entered one house, I saw several women working in the kitchen. I asked for food and they gave me some and a cup of coffee. How delicious this tasted. I made myself comfortable at the warm stove; took my shoes off and dried my wet socks.

The women didn't ask me any questions, but half an hour later, the man of the house walked in. Right away he asked me for papers. I told him that I didn't have any, and he left. Half an hour later, he came back with a Russian soldier and a Czech Militiaman.

The Russian shoved his submachinegun into my face.

"Hands up."

He shouted and then interrogated me, after he had made sure that I was unarmed. I had to empty my pockets. The Russian laid my bandage aside, but the Czech opened it up and my watch fell out. The Russian grabbed it for himself. He was very suspicious and it took me about twenty minutes to convince him that I was Russian. I had to go with them to another village. It was dark already and I was locked into a barn. I crawled into the hay and soon was asleep.

When I woke up the next morning, I saw the whole barn was full of German soldiers. These were the stragglers they had rounded up in the area, and two Russian horsemen were bringing them to a prison camp in Budweis. Didn't I hear that name before?

On to Budweis with the German captives. But there was also a Russian civilian with us who had papers to prove what I was claiming to be. We walked for a while together. After escaping for the ninth day and without proper nutrition, I was weak on my feet. One of the soldiers got off his horse and let me ride it. I was not used to that and soon was sore. So I got off and, holding onto the saddle strap, let the horse pull me along. This made walking much easier.

We had to walk all day without any food. Late at night we arrived at Budweis. It was drizzling. I found a soaked piece of bread stomped into the mud. I picked it up and ate it. We were locked into a barn overnight.

We were assembled outside next morning. The soldiers came back with an officer. They approached me and the Russian civilian, and the Captain said;
> *"Now I hear that you two fellows are Russian. I need my soldiers here, so I am going to give you the order to bring those German prisoners to another prison camp in Austria."*

I was stunned, but stayed cool. They gave us food rations and marching papers, and we moved out with about 200 German soldiers. They could have taken off any time they wanted. They could have killed us; we had no weapons. The Germans were so demoralized that they walked along like sheep. We got into Austria, which was friendly country for me. Whenever we reached a village, the Germans were going into the houses, looking for food. Did anybody escape? I don't know.

On the way one time we were stopped by a Russian Army officer. After we had shown the marching papers, we could move on. I had to make a decision, because I had no business at the next camp so when we got into a wooded area, I just left the column and vanished into the woods.

I got to an Austrian village and asked the farmer for shelter. I told him that I was German. He agreed reluctantly to hide me in his barn until dark. He was afraid of the Russians in the village. I was also worried that my escape was discovered by now and they might be looking for me. When it got dark, the farmer brought me some food which I wolfed down, and I was on my way.

It was a dark night. Soon I was in a forest again. I walked along a trail but clouds moved in and I could not get my bearings any more. I began worrying that I might walk into Czechoslovakia again. Suddenly I heard the sounds of sheep ahead. As I got near, I saw a campfire behind the trees. I was glad that somebody was out here; a shepherd that I could ask for directions.

Spoils of War?

When I arrived at the campfire, nobody was around. I set down and waited. Suddenly I felt a rifle in my back. I had walked into a Russian camp. They were former prisoners of war, held by the Germans. Freed now, they were walking home and taking with them 5,000 sheep.

After I had explained to them who I was, they didn't believe me. They didn't let me leave. Next morning, they hitched up a wagon and drove me to Army headquarters. There I stayed firm and stuck to my story. At least they gave me something to eat.

In the afternoon a soldier showed up. Pointing with his submachine gun the direction, I had to walk ahead of him. My mind was racing. Was he taking me somewhere to shoot me? After all, I had violated the curfew. When we came to the last house in the village, he motioned me to wait. He came back with his commander. The Captain interrogated me again, and finally said:

"I will believe you, but don't walk around any more at night. We almost have shot you as a spy. Go to the town of Gmund and report at the camp where they collect all foreigners and send them home."

I was glad to get away again. Now I gave up the idea to get to the American side. On the way to Gmund, I collected some discarded clothing in a forest. I found underwear, shirts and also a knapsack. I didn't have to travel light anymore

At the refugee camp in Gmund, I registered as a Pole. I had decided to go home and find out what happened to my parents and the family farm. I got living quarters in an abandoned apartment. Food we were served in the camp. After three weeks of hardships, starving and running, I felt like in a sanitarium. With regular food, I was getting back my strength. I was exploring some abandoned houses in the neighborhood. I found three brand new fur jackets to wear under other clothing. This was a treasure which I put away in my knapsack. Later in winter it would be of good use to me.

One day I went to the nearby highway and I saw a large column of German prisoners walking by under Russian escort. Not long ago I was marching in such a column. Suddenly I recognized the uniforms some were wearing; this was the bunch I had escaped from! Any moment my Comrades could show up. I could take no chances. I stood up and walked away. Danger was still lurking around me.

After 4 weeks, a transport brought us by rail to Pressburg. In the camp were many nationalities - Jugoslavs, Russians, Poles and French also - all people displaced by the Germans. I felt uneasy here. One slip-up could put me in jeopardy. They would have lynched me if they recognized me as a German.

I was reminded of that some weeks later, when a transport was leaving for Poland. A young man was recognized by a Russian officer as a German. He had stood to attention, as we Germans did, when an officer spoke to us. The Russian pulled his gun and was hitting the lad repeatedly over the head. Then he was taken away.

On the way to Poland, nothing much happened. After arriving, rumor spread that we were bound for another camp. I didn't like this much and I left the transport. I joined four men who had been in the German concentration camp Mauthausen. Their heads were shaved and they had numbers tattooed on their arms. We boarded an overcrowded streetcar and for a while I was separated from my companions. At the next station, a Polish Militiaman boarded and began checking ID's. All Germans were arrested and taken off the car

When he asked me, I said that I was from a concentration camp and my companions confirmed it - and I got away.

We went to the train station. There we found out that we needed a special permit from the Red Cross to board the train. We went to the Red Cross. My companions just showed their convict number and received permits.

When it was my turn at the counter, the young girl at the counter asked me my name, since I had no number to show. I said my name was Jerzy, which meant George in Polish. Then she looked at me and smiling, she asked,

"You mean Georg?"

Which was the German equivalent. I just smiled back at her. Then she wanted to know how come I still had my long, wavy hair.

"Because I wasn't there long enough."

I responded. She gave me the paper.

At the train station, people were crowding the departing train. When we wanted to board it turned out, our permits were not accepted. I went to the front of the train. Behind the locomotive was a baggage car. This minute the mail arrived to be loaded on the train. I did not hesitate and helped loading the mail. When done, I threw my knapsack in too, and boarded. I found a hiding place behind the parcels. Soon the train left, and I was on my last leg home.

I was thinking - what would I find at home? My mother and grandmother had escaped in January 1945, when the Russian Army was approaching. Driving a team of horses, they made it to Germany. In spite of that, they were attacked on the way and overrun by the Russian Army. My father was not home at that time. After attending my wedding in Berlin, he had to go to Posen on business. He never made it back home. The Russians started their last offensive on Berlin.

Miraculously my parents found each other six weeks later in the city of Cottbus. My wife wrote all this to me in her last letter.

At 2 o'clock in the morning, I arrived at my destination. I got off the train in Piotrkov. Here I had attended high school before the war. Because of curfew time, the station was locked up and nobody could leave until morning. Anxiously I moved on. I had to walk twenty-five kilometers. The closer I came, the more nervous I got. One more hill and behind it I would see our farm. Was it still there? Or was it destroyed? When I saw the roofs I was relieved.

When I arrived at the gate, I saw nobody outside. I went to the house and opened the door. I saw several pairs of shoes lined up along the wall. When I noticed a pair of child's shoes I knew that my parents were not here. I knocked and a strange woman answered the door. She let me in and I asked for water. She told me that the farmer was not here. She was German and had to work here. She told me that the farmer was just the caretaker of the farm because the previous owners did not return.

When the farmer arrived, he recognized me. He said that I shouldn't have come back. All German men were arrested by the Militia. I stayed and next morning, I went to town to report at the Militia post. The farmer went with me. He wanted to speak for me, but was dismissed at the gate. I was taken inside a room for interrogation.

In the rooms were several tables with vices mounted to them. I saw also several rubber clubs and I knew what that meant. Here the Germans were beaten and quite often killed during the interrogations.

They knew right away who I was. I was the *'German teacher's son'* who was flying with the Luftwaffe. They wanted to know if it was me who tried to bomb the town in the last days of the war.

"What war medals did you earn?"
They asked. When I told them that I had two *Iron Crosses* one man snarled at me,
"Now we will give you a wooden cross!"

He hit me in the chest with his fist. He wanted to do it again, but his superior stopped him. Strangely enough, I was not beaten any more.

In the afternoon, I was taken to prison and locked in a solitary cell. When the prisoners were taken for a walk in the evening, I saw the yard had a brick wall. All around were bullet marks. This meant that many people were lined up against it and shot. This was not encouraging.

The other prisoners were Polish criminals. Every day, their families had to bring them food because the prison did not supply food. How was I to survive? The prisoners had some compassion and shared some food with me.

One night a riot broke out. I heard shots and several prisoners escaped.

One day was like the other. I lay most of the time on the floor. There was no bed in the cell. Under the ceiling there was a small window with bars. Once I heard an airplane and then I saw it fly by high above. It looked like a Heinkel. How I wished I was in it.

In the second week, they brought another German prisoner into my cell. I knew him from the bicycle shop where my father had bought me a bike. He had served with the Kriegsmarine and just returned. We were talking about past times for two days, then they took him away. Later I found out that they had shot him afterwards. He had to dig his own grave. He had not harmed anybody during the war. My fate was uncertain, but I stayed calm.

After two weeks, I was bailed out by the farmer who was on our farm. It was a good feeling to be outside again and with people. It was just harvest time and I helped to bring in the harvest.

It was strange to be on our farm. Most of it was still like at our time, only it didn't belong to us anymore. The Polish government had disowned us collectively for helping the Germans during the war.

Did we have a choice? The Poles had made the choice for us when they killed 49,000 VolksDeutsche (Germans living in Poland) in the weeks before the war began. I had lost four of my family then.

I should have escaped then because it was easy. But this was my home and I did not want to leave - at least not yet. This was a mistake.

Two weeks later, a Militiaman came and arrested me. I ended up in prison again. The Poles were rounding up all German men who were still on the loose. They marched us off to the concentration camp at Piotrkov. Next day we had to line up in the yard. An officer came to inspect us. He looked at each one of us in the face. When he looked at me, he turned to his men and told them to watch me closely because I would escape, given a chance. He had pegged me right.

After a few days, we were turned over to the Russian Komandantura and locked in a cellar. In the afternoon, a Sergeant came and asked if anybody was an auto mechanic. I volunteered right away although I was no mechanic. I just knew how to drive, but I could stay and the other prisoners were shipped to Russia.

It looked pretty good for me. I was free to move around and having the same food and quarters as the soldiers. I had to drive the officers around in a flashy red Mercedes convertible; sometimes to different cities. One time we drove to my home town. I talked the Russian into driving to our nearby farm. Did the Poles look when I drove up! They had to give us a basket with apples and were quite mad about it. This was the last time I saw our farm.

On the 6th of August the A-Bomb was dropped. Japan surrendered and World War Two was over. After six months, my good time at the Komandantura came to a sudden end. The Russians didn't need me anymore and turned me over to the Polish Militia.

The Russian Komisar had hated me because I had challenged him several times, when he was making stupid demands regarding work. Twice I made him so mad that he pulled his gun on me. With a Russian, one never could be sure when he would pull the trigger.

If he did, nobody would have asked any questions. When it came to German prisoners, the Russians were masters over life and death at that time.

At the Militia Post, I could not move around freely anymore. Most of the time we were under supervision of a guard. We worked on cars and motorcycles in the garage. I figured out how to get a BMW motorcycle running and many times I drove around town alone, pretending to test drive. I should have taken off - I didn't, because this was also home. Here I had gone to school for seven years. Here I had dated my first girls. Here were many memories of my youth.

One Sunday afternoon, Fate struck me a blow. I went to visit a German prisoner at the Komandantura. He told me that he was homesick and he would escape at night with a German woman as an interpreter. Would I like to come along? I declined, since it was still cold and snow outside.

Next morning, all hell broke loose at our Militia post. The Russians were there and the Komisar was shouting, asking for me. He accused me of knowing about the escape plan of the German prisoner. Since I didn't report it, he punished me by sending me to the Concentration Camp at Lodz. The Poles arrested me immediately and drove me to Lodz.

They delivered me to the dreaded Polish Secret Police (like the Russian *NKVD*). I was interrogated all day long. When I told them that I was flying with the Luftwaffe. The interpreter mentioned to the other men,
'Here you see a man who killed thousands of innocent people.'

Finally, after debating for a while, they decided that they could use me as a mechanic. I ended up in the concentration camp where they kept seventy-five other German prisoners. There I spent fourteen months at hard labor. We had to work 16 hours a day, restoring German cars from the war. We were fed only one quart of bean soup a day, and 100 kg of bread.

One time I was accused of sabotaging a Russian officer's car I had worked on. It had lost a wheel. One of the men in the camp had sabotaged me. He was jealous because his girlfriend, who was in charge of the kitchen, was giving me favors.

The Komandant threatened me with hanging if it happened again. Another time I was beaten up by a guard for no reason. After this incident I decided to escape. In the night of the 28th of May 1947, I broke out under the nose of the Militia guard.

When I was coming home from work that evening, I saw a ladder left on the ground by the workers who had worked on the roof. This was my ticket out. It took past midnight until all men in the room were asleep. I dressed and sneaked outside.

First I had to find out where the guard was. He could have been making his round inside the workshop, or could be sitting in his guardhouse. I waited a while and when I could not see him, I went over to the shop and hid behind a car.

At that moment, the guard came across the yard from the guardhouse. I thought that he had spotted me but no, he just stood in front of the car, smoking a cigarette. Finally he went back to his guardhouse. Now I had to make my final decision........

It was FREEDOM or DEATH.

I grabbed the ladder and walked in full view across the yard. I set up the ladder against a roof and climbed up. Along the roof's edge I crawled over to the guardhouse. From there I reached the street. I jumped to the ground and walked away quickly.

The street was empty because of curfew time. As I rushed on, suddenly I noticed two Militiamen approaching on the other side of the street. I thought that I'd had it, but they were so busy talking that they didn't notice me.

I moved on to a streetcar stop. With the first car, I left Lodz. At the next town, I disembarked, went to the highway and flagged down a truck. I gave the driver twenty-five Zloty and he took me along. I sat in the back, on top of crates and we moved quickly along.

I was holding on for my life and was not paying attention what was going on along the highway behind us. As I looked up, I saw our Komandant's blue Fiat only thirty yards behind us! I ducked behind a crate. At that moment, we had to stop because of a checkpoint. The car drove up beside us. Now I was waiting; they would come and get me. Nothing happened.

I heard the car drive on and then my truck. I had been incredibly lucky. We arrived at the town of Kalisz and I got off. This was halfway to Breslau, my destination.

I went to the train station. I saw Militiamen outside, so I had to be careful. I needed a train ticket, but I didn't dare walk past the Militiamen; so I went to a travel bureau instead and bought it there. Then I went back to the station and waited some distance away.

I could see the train, and when I saw it pull out, I ran like hell and just could catch it. Nobody had time to stop me. I found a seat, hoping there would be no controls on the way. I arrived without incident at Breslau around midnight.

Next day I went by train to Liegnitz. This was a little closer to the border. In Liegnitz I found out that there was no train to the border and that the bridge across the river Oder was guarded. What now?

I remembered that I had an address of some German people living in Breslau. Maybe they could help me? I returned to Breslau, arriving past midnight. It was curfew and we had to leave the station. I just kept on moving. The city was in ruins. Breslau was the city I had supplied from the air.

At the station, I got a general direction to my address. It was pitch dark; I was looking for a house number. Were there no houses undamaged? I was just following my instincts and found the street.

As I walked along, I met a Militiaman. I approached him and asked for the house I was looking for. He had a flashlight and we found the house. Incredibly he didn't ask me any questions. I thanked him and he moved on.

The house was badly damaged, so I decided to wait till next morning. I lay down on wooden boards and fell asleep. Next morning I found out that the people I was looking for had been settled out a few weeks ago. Back to Square one - to Liegnitz!

After arriving there. I had to find shelter so I would be off the streets. I was watching the people. When I walked up to some older woman chatting at the street corner, I heard German.

I asked if they would know somebody who would take me in, for pay of course. They gave me an address and I went there. A man took me in for several days, after I had given him the rest of my money.

Next morning, I went to the city hall. I had heard that people were going there to register, to be settled out to Germany. I saw a young woman coming, holding several passports in her hands. I asked her if she could slip my name in when registering. After a while, she came back smiling. *She had my TRAIN TICKET!*

The few days went by quickly. On the day of departure, I went to the station. Lots of people, mostly women, children and old men were waiting. But no man of my young age of 27. Suddenly I saw a Militiaman approaching me. *Could something go wrong in the last minute???*

He wanted to know what I had in my pockets. I had a knife and a comb. He took the knife and walked away. This was my last tribute to my enemies. When the train was leaving, I was relieved. My long Odyssee was over and I had my freedom!!!

In East Germany we had to stay for three weeks in a quarantine camp. They gave me a new ID card. I called my wife and she arrived a few days later. We had not seen each other for two and a half years after our wedding. We went home together. My parents had found refuge in a small village near Torgau. Food was scarce. My mother helped out in the kitchen of an estate. Father had been working as a translator for the Russian Army. They were dismantling all industrial plants and shipping them back to Russia.

Later my father was teaching the Russian language in German schools. It was a hard life for him and he never got over the loss of our family farm. He was ailing and died in January 1955.

After harvest, we were going on the fields and collected the grain left on the ground and digging up the remaining potatoes. On this we just existed. There were no jobs.

I was recuperating from my ordeals, trying to forget the war and prison. But the nightmares didn't stop. Each night when I went to sleep, I was reliving combat and the escapes.

Again I was running and running, ducking machine gun bullets. Burning planes were falling from the sky and crashing around me. It took years until this nightmare stopped.

For six months I was left alone. Then in February 1948 I received a letter from the State employment office. I was to report there at the city of Torgau. We had heard rumors that the Communists were taking men to the Uranium mines at Aue. Because of the radiation, people were dying there like flies. Many men were also shipped for forced labor to Russia.

When I found the office, I saw that it was the Department of Mining. I knew enough. I turned on my heels and went home packing. Same afternoon, I was on a train to West Germany. I knew that the police would come looking for me next day. I was on the run again.

When the train arrived at the boarder, it was about 11 at night. Many people left the train. Since we were crossing the border illegally, we had to walk around the border checkpoint. I followed the crowd. They appeared to know their way, but soon we were stopped by the Volkspolizei (East German Border Patrol) already waiting. We were all arrested and brought to the station. Next morning we had to chop wood for them as punishment.

The following morning we were loaded on a train and brought to another post. There they interrogated us. The West Germans were sorted out and released. The East Germans had to pay a 50 RM fine and were sent home.

When I was paying my fine, I could see through the window; two West Germans crossing into West Germany. So when I got outside, I just followed them and nobody stopped me.

At the next train station, I boarded a train to Köln (Cologne). My former radioman lived there. I had received a letter from him that he was home from Russian captivity. He had spent eighteen months in a prison camp.

He saw our gunner, Uffz. Schulz die from the hardships. When he too got very sick, the Russians released him. My wartime comrade gave me shelter for 3 weeks.

I went to a refugee camp and registered with the authorities as a political refugee from the Communists. They gave me an ID card as a resident of the British Occupation Zone. With this I got the *Zuzugsgenehimigung* (permission to live and get a job) in the area of Köln. So equipped, I went back illegally to East Germany to fetch my pregnant wife. This time I went alone across the border and was not caught. We packed my wife's possessions and left the second day, because it was not safe for me to be here.

We said good bye to my mother; my father was not home. My wife wanted to say good bye to her mother, so we traveled to Berlin first. We picked up a few more things and left for the border. We had to cross illegally at Helmstedt. Again we left the train and followed the crowd through the fields. As we waded through the deep snow, soon we lost sight of the people who traveled light. I was carrying two suitcases, a rucksack on my back with a suitcase on top and two bicycle wheels around my neck. My wife, eight months pregnant, couldn't carry anything.

We followed a path into a forest when we met up with a crowd. It was the people from the train, who had already been arrested by Russian soldiers. We had to turn back too. Since I had to carry so much, we were holding everybody back. I overheard one soldier telling the other to search us. They were looking for contraband - booze and weapons. Since we had none, they let us go because I now had a West German ID card.

We continued our journey into West Germany. At the next train station, we boarded the train to Köln. It was in March 1948 when we arrived in the FREE WORLD!!

CHAPTER 25

Flying Combat with the *Luftwaffe IV*
More from Member ROLF ZYDEK.

It is summer 1943. The young Unteroffizier Hans Seyringer has just left the Flying school (Jagdfliegerschule) and was sent to II./JG27 with only 200 hours of flying in his FB (FlugBuch, or Flight logbook). II./JG 27 had just been relocated from the Mediterranean Theater of war and we led by the very successful Major Werner Schroer.

Hans Seyringer received a brand new Me 109 G-6 armed with one 30mm cannon and two 13mm guns, and two underwing 20mm cannons. Being heavily armed like this, the Me 109 G-6 was a very sensitive aircraft. In addition, an underbelly fuel tank was fitted. Just getting this *'monster'* into the air, needs very experienced hands on the stick especially when taking off. Thus equipped, the Me 109 was totally unqualified for dogfighting other fighters.

In spite of the additional belly tank, the short range of the Me 109 was always a major problem. Therefore, the four squadrons of the group were specially parked on a circular road of Wiesbaden Airport so that all squadrons, groups or just two plane formations could take off at the very same time and get into formation already in the air.

This sometimes led to strange situations with rocket-armed Me 109's (some of the fighters were equipped with two rocket tubes containing two 210mm rockets in place of the two 20mm wing guns). Sometimes these rocket-armed fighters released their rockets by mistake, due to the very bad ground conditions and the narrow gear track of the 109, which makes the airplane bouncing, jumping up and down.

Because of the very special takeoff position, some squadrons took off facing each other. These rockets now roared just a few yards above or very nearby the opposite squadron taking off. Although there wasn't any damage caused, the situation was quite frightening at least, for one group of fighters.

For his very first mission, Seyringer was assigned to one of the experts as wingman, and told to stay as close to him as possible and not to lose him at all times. As soon as the bombers were in range, the Squadron Leader decided about the way and manner of attack. This was basically depending on the experience of that pilot and the attack situation.

Seyringer remembers that three or four times they did a head-on attack, but found it most disappointing. The time you need to overtake a bomber squadron, turn around, aim at them and just have a split second to fire was in no way worth the whole attack.

The more common method, and much more loved by the less experienced pilots, was the good old little higher 6 o'clock position (from behind and slightly higher) with a four-ship element, either behind each other or in echelon formation. Then after the attack, the four-ship element became a pair of two-ship elements as they banked away to different sides for regrouping and a possible second attack.

It was often discussed by pilots of JG 27 to attack from below, as the bombers represent the biggest target this way. But mainly the loss of speed when turning away and thus the slow speed, gave the gunners in the B-17 with their .50 caliber guns, a pleasant target, so this idea was soon scrapped.

29 Jan 1944, 800 American B-17 Flying Fortress Fortresses and B-24 Liberators attacked Frankfurt/Main. A similar attack followed a day later to Brunswick (Braunschweig). Hans Seyringer, an expert now, was again at the controls of an Me 109 G-6 to defend his home country. His group took off and they intercepted the bombers over the Baltic Sea. He remembers the action this way:

"Our group formed and we prepared a nice attack from behind. Whilst closing in to the bomber formation, we were already expected by some nasty hails of bullets and we already had our first losses even before we came to shoot. Have you ever tried to take a shower and tried not to get wet? Well, this best described the situation when closing in to a bomber formation of that kind and being awaited by the rear gunners.

I always chose those bombers flying most outside at the left or right side, as the defensive fire here was not as bad as in the middle of the formation. I aimed at the first B-17 from about 430 yards, a distance quite okay for my big guns.

I saw several hits on the bomber, but it didn't fall down. So I swung around for a second attack, but I realized that my wingman was gone. These youngsters didn't have those nerves of steel to stay to the bombers that close. Anyway, whilst looking for him, I saw two P-47s escorting the bombers above me and shimmering into the sun. They couldn't see me yet, so I decided a surprise attack.

I banked into position behind them and released all of my guns and saw how the engine of the one Thunderbolt immediately caught fire, whilst the other went away into a deep dive. Should I follow him or stay again at the bombers? My brain was working, but not for long. A second flight of two P-47s dived onto my Me 109, firing from all 16 guns!!!

Suddenly I heard a terrible BANG in the fuselage and my 109 was trembling and shaking like hell. My rudder didn't respond, my stick was non-existing and I smelled smoke from the front. I even saw a little fire from the engine nacelle and heard a big explosion in the cockpit. It looked like my own 30mm ammo was exploding, and this was the time to bail out - *quickly*.

I felt that I was injured somewhere in the back and at my arm. Blood was running down my left arm in this strange, warm manner and I was anxious that I might not get out of my plane in time but after a while, pushing and pulling, the canopy went away and the slipstream ripped me out of my seat. I immediately pulled my parachute; then I lost my consciousness.

I woke up in a Dutch hospital with some terrible headache, a paralyzed left arm and some bigger scratches to my back."

This was Hans Seyringer's report of his last mission over the Reich. He was out of the war.

The appearance of American fighter escorts over the Reich shocked the German Fighter HQ. When this was reported to Luftwaffe Chief Hermann Göring, he first made jokes about it and even reprimanded the responsible officer for air reconnaissance.

Photo - Luftwaffe Commander in Chief Hermann Göring.

Even later when there were no doubts of P-47, P-38 and P-51 fighters as bomber escorts over Germany, Göring declared that all his pilots were blind and said they should attack the bombers and not any fictitious *'phantom fighters'*.

The result of this was an ironical statement by one of the German Kommandeure which best described the situation:

'There is nothing safer in German skies than American fighter escorts.'

CHAPTER 26

Ivan Kuzhedub – Top Soviet ACE

From Member GEORGE CHANDLER.

EDITOR NOTE – GEORGE CHANDLER is an **ACE** with five confirmed aerial victories in his P-38 Lightning in the skies of the Pacific. He was attached to the squadron that shot down Admiral Isoruku Yamamoto although he was not in that killing flight.

He writes about the top scoring **ACE** of the Soviet Union and in fact, the top **ACE** of all the Allied Air Forces.

Ivan was born 8 June 1920 and was the fifth child born into a poor peasant family in the village of Obrazheyevka, Sumy Region in Ukraine. In 1938 he entered an aviation school. In the beginning in the fall of that year he was appointed an instructor at the same school, much to his

disappointment. He wanted to be a fighter pilot and not a teacher. He flew a lot, experimenting and perfecting his piloting skills. He said;
 'I would have never left the plane if I could have.'

 'I greatly enjoyed improving my piloting skills and aerobatics' he wrote later.

In 1941, Germany invaded the USSR. Kozhedub submitted numerous requests to his commanders to send him to the front. However, it was only late fall of 1942 that he, together with other instructors and graduates of the school, was sent to the 240th Fighter Regiment. In August 1942, this regiment was one of the first to be equipped with the new Lavochkin LA-5 fighter, pictured here. However, the pilots were retrained to fly those planes in a hurry - just in 15 days.

Pilots and their new Lavochkin LA-5 Fighters

As a result, the regiment incurred heavy losses in fierce fighting and ten days later, it was withdrawn from the front. However, losses embitter the heart and kindle hatred in it, a feeling much stronger than the passion and resolve to win. It mobilizes the mind and physical potential for the ultimate defeat of the Germans.

In late December 1942, pilots began to fly missions again. *'Dub'* flew together with his constant supporting plane partner (wingman) Mukhin and shot down his first German plane. This was in the Battle of Kursk.

Kozhedub shot down 62 German planes in 120 air battles in 330 combat missions. On 19 February 1945, when Kozhedub and the pilot of a

supporting aircraft (Dmitry Titarenko) were flying a mission over the Oder River, they met an Me 262, one of the world's first jet fighters. Kozhedub plunged his plane down from above, sneaked up on the German from behind and below, and shot him down.

At the time of the Korean War, Ivan Kozhedub had commanded the 324th Soviet Air Division that arrived in Korea in November 1951 and had flown the MIG-15 fighters.

For his efforts in World War II, he became one of only three men to earn three **GOLD STARS** (Hero of the Soviet Union), the highest award in the USSR. He died in 1991, covered with glory.

About the Author

Born and raised in Chicago and the western suburbs, Harry Cooper joined the US Air Force right out of high school. After six months intensive training is special weapons (hydrogen bombs) at Lowry Air Force Base (Denver) he was mis-assigned to Chanute Air Force only 100 miles from his home. To his very good luck, he was assigned to the base swimming pool as a lifeguard, working one day on and one day off, making it was easy to go home every second day. When the summer ended, he was transferred to an active base and was assigned to the 98th Bomb Wing at Lincoln Air Force Base just outside Lincoln, Nebraska.

After spending two and a half years working with special weapons and since he always wanted to be a fighter pilot, he applied for Officer Candidate School as he neared his 21st birthday. He was the only one of 30 who passed the tough two-day long battery of tests and he was assigned an OCS class. His pilot's physical gave him a clean slate to fly, but luck was not with him. The Air Force was so overloaded with pilots from World War II and Korea that Air Cadets was shut down. He could be an officer but not a pilot.

He was then honorably discharged from the Air Force and went to college where he earned his BS in Business Administration and began his career in the Chicago area. Since he could not enter aerial combat, he chose the next best thing – he went into auto racing! He first tried his hand at drag racing and while driving for a friend, he was Class Champion 11 times out of 22 – pretty good. But the following year, he drove his own car and out of the next 26 weeks, he was Class Champion 26 times and Little Stock Eliminator four times, setting some national records along the way.

Then his heart turned to the oval tracks and after three successful years at the short tracks around Chicago, where he also gave the racing news on the "Motorsports International" television show, he moved up to the big tracks and raced against A. J. Foyt, the Unser Brothers, Johnny Rutherford and other great racers. He was a Feature Editor at *Stock Car Racing Magazine* during his racing years doing 'behind the wheel' racing reports as well as monthly columns for major American and Australian racing magazines and was an executive for a Chicago firm.

Things changed drastically for him in 1976. His crew chief left for a job in the normal world, his assistant crew chief quit to open his own auto parts store and his best crew member quit to join the Air Force. While running the 1976 Texas 500 in the lead pack, his engine blew! On the way back to Chicago, the engine in the transporter truck blew. It was not a good sign. The final straw was when he got to the office the next day and found that his superior had left the company and his new boss was a corporate executive for whom Harry had no respect. It was time for a major change!

previous page: Flotilla Commander Harry Cooper, US Coast Guard (Aux.). Below right, Cooper's #17 is passing #19 at about 190mph; 1976 Texas 500.

It really was time for a major change, so Harry sold everything, bought a 30-foot sailing yacht and went to live the quiet life in the Florida Keys and the Bahamas. This was to change his life and in fact, the history of the War At Sea itself. It was there that he became interested in the U-Bootwaffe.

While cruising in the southern Bahamas, Harry stopped at a strange island that had been a working plantation during the war years. There were the ruins of a mansion atop a hill, the remains of a barracks building and a radio shack nearby. The caretaker told him a few German U-Boats had stopped there for fresh water during the war. That put the hook in Harry and once he returned to Chicago, he began to research the U-Boat portion of WW II and has become the world's preeminent expert on the subject.

Returning to the business world, he became Regional Vice President for a major company in Chicago but founded Sharkhunters in 1983. By mid-1987, he realized that it would be impossible to keep a regular job and then spend all the time necessary to contact the veterans, dig in the files, visit the veterans to interview them and all the other tasks necessary to preserving this history honestly. He made a tough decision.

On a Friday, he turned in the keys to his 12 offices around Illinois and quit his high-paying executive job, just two weeks after getting a nice raise in salary. His wife of just two years was most surprised with this decision and even more surprised (maybe even shocked) to learn that they were moving to Florida to do this research full time and at no salary. She was not convinced at all, since they were to have their first child in less than 4 months now there was no insurance, no security - but this had to be done!

Fortunately, it succeeded and Sharkhunters has the great distinction of being the preeminent source for the history of the WW II U-Bootwaffe.

Harry was a member of the Adventurer's Club in Chicago (Editor of the newsletter), member of the Chicago Press Club and the International Press Club of Chicago. He wrote several books including "***Sponsorship***" as a guide for racers to get sponsorship and he wrote "***1001 Things to do in Florida for Free***".

Harry is listed in "*Who's Who in America*" as well as in "*Who's Who of American Business Leaders*" and in 2006 was nominated as "Man of the Year" by the American Biographical Institute. He spent twelve years with the United States Coast Guard (Aux.) achieving the position of Flotilla Commander with a rank similar to a full Lieutenant. With this research, Harry has met and become friends with most of the surviving Skippers, many of the officers and crewmen from the U-Bootwaffe as well as American sub vets and world leaders from the US, the Soviet Union and modern day Russia.

Sharkhunters' Credits

Founded in 1983, Sharkhunters International is recognized as the only official worldwide publication source of information on German U-Boat history. The U-Boat Skippers, officers and many crewmen worked with Sharkhunters to give their knowledge and their memories so that the real history will continue. Sharkhunters has done productions for various television shows including the History Channel as well as assisting many authors write highly accurate and well acclaimed books.

BBC reporter Graham Pound stated that Sharkhunters are:
"The most respected and most authoritative source in the world for U-Boat history."

Reporter Adam Harcourt-Webster said that;
"Sharkhunters are <u>THE</u> experts on the U-Boats."

In addition, Sharkhunters has helped many authors with their works:
  "Operation Drumbeat" by Professor Michael Gannon
  "Torpedoes in the Gulf" by Melanie Wiggins
  "Critical Mass" by Carter Hydrick
  "Hitler's Ashes" by Col. Howard Buechner
…..to name just a few. These authors were all Sharkhunters Members.

Sharkhunters has also assisted in productions for:
  The History Channel
  Ghost Hunters International

About Sharkhunters

Founded in February 1983, Sharkhunters International is the first, the best and the only accurate source of published history on the U-Bootwaffe. The reason is simple; the data not only comes from official files and documents but it also comes from the memories of those who lived this war. The top Skippers, many of the officers and crewmen of the U-Bootwaffe were participating Members as were a great many Allied personnel including the four Medal of Honor American submarine Skippers of the war.

Fluckey   O'Kane   Ramage   Street

Many other great men were Members of Sharkhunters including these;

Kretschmer   Topp   Hardegen   Hess

RONALD REAGAN was a Sharkhunters Member from 1991 until his passing.

Let us send a complimentary copy of our **KTB** Magazine for your inspection. Send an email to us at **sharkhunters@earthlink.net**, tell us your name (first & last); by return email, you'll be reading our **KTB** Magazine.

Harry Cooper   *When Eagles Soared*

Sharkhunters 'Patrols' and 'Expeditions'

In addition to publishing the most historically accurate information on the history of the U-Bootwaffe and the men who fought the war on both sides, Sharkhunters also organizes tours to many historic places for our Members. For instance:

Bunker Patrol from Berlin east to Warsaw.

Destroyed HQ of the OKW   **Abandoned fortress in Poland**

Gun bunker overlooking the Baltic   **Wolfsschanze (Wolf's Lair)**

Sharkhunters does not merely use files and documents in our research but we go to the places where this history took place. We videotape, shoot still photos and we walk in the footsteps of history. During this *'Patrol'* we slept in the SS officers' barracks at Hitler's Wolfsschanze, the Wolf's Lair, where the assassination attempt was made on Hitler in 1944. Sharkhunters was there.

The Southern Redoubt/Fortress Area

The Allies feared the leaders of the Reich would make a desperate last ditch stand in the Bavarian Alps at the Obersalzberg with its bunkers, tunnels and fortifications, some of which are still undiscovered today.

Coal bunkers   **Hitler's tunnel**   **Göring's bunker entrance**

Northern Germany

At the U-Boat Memorial   **The Skipper at the Periscope**

With the veterans   **At the submarine *U-995***

Harry Cooper *When Eagles Soared*

The Reich Moves to South America
And our Sharkhunters "*Patrols*" follow them…..

…..to an island in the southern Atlantic vacated by Brazil in 1938 for the use of the Kriegsmarine in the early stages of the war then again at the end of the war, including this radio facility built in 1938.

1938 German photo   2009 photo by the author

Who lived here in Argentina?

In this manor house?   In this eerie hotel?

We know the answers to these questions because our Sharkhunters groups have been here. You may join Sharkhunters for any of our expeditions; check the website for details. You may also read all about the move by the leaders of the Reich to this area in our book "*Escape from the Bunker*" which is also available from Sharkhunters. Check the website for details.

What Else From Sharkhunters?

We do more here at Sharkhunters – much more. Log onto our website at www.sharkhunters.com and see all that is featured there – such as:

- Books – many more books are listed;
- DVDs – almost 200 different titles covering:
    Combat action on land – tanks, artillery, infantry
    Aerial combat – much from gun cameras
    Submarine warfare of several countries
    Personal interviews with many WW II veterans
    Great films by Sharkhunters Member **LENI RIEFENSTAHL**
    Different looks at life before the war as well as during
    Training films to fly various USAAF fighters and bombers
    Much more………….take a moment to check them out

- Hand signed, limited edition fine art prints
- Coffee mugs with conning tower emblems
- Coffee mugs with veterans photos
- T-Shirts with conning tower emblems
- Hand signed photographs of veterans
- CDs of music of the war years – German, Russian etc
- CDs of interviews with WW II U-Boat Skippers

Naturally you will read all the details on becoming a Member of Sharkhunters – receiving a free hand signed photo of a veteran, our 44 page KTB Magazine ten times annually, discounts on any items offered by Sharkhunters and you will see all about our:

Sharkhunters *'Patrols'*…..you can join us in Germany, France, Austria, Argentina, Chile and any of the other fascinating places we go AND into places off limits to everyone else. Check the website.

Other Books by Harry Cooper

"Sponsorship" was written when Harry was driving the high banks and was a Feature Editor for Stock Car Racing Magazine. It was a "How To" book for motor racers to secure sponsorships for their racing efforts. Out of print.

"1001 Things to do in Florida for Free" great for Florida visitors. Out of print.

"Escape from the Bunker" relates the historically accurate escape of Hitler, Eva Braun, Martin Bormann and many other high ranking figures of the Third Reich with top secret Abwehr and Kriegsmarine charts as well as files from the OSS, FBI and various other Intel organizations. **Available from Sharkhunters.**

"U-BOAT!" volume I is the beginning of this work with many stories from the men of the U-Bootwaffe. **Available from Sharkhunters.**

"U-BOAT!" volume II is further history of the U-Bootwaffe with many stories from the men of the U-Bootwaffe. **Available from Sharkhunters.**

"Rise and Fall of the U-Bootwaffe" tells how the German Navy secretly designed, built and tested submarines in a neutral country at a time when Germany was to have nothing to do with submarines. This book tells of the new types, the construction, what U-Boats were in combat sinking ships long before World War Two began on 1 September 1939. There is much more, but it ends with the lengthy debriefing of Großadmiral Karl Dönitz. He tells all – why they were so successful in the early days of the war; what changed; how it affected the U-Bootwaffe as well as the other branches of the Wehrmacht and ultimately why Germany lost the war. He also answers the oft asked question – if he had plans to defect to the Soviet Union at any point. **Available from Sharkhunters.**

Send an email to sharkhunters@earthink.net with your name and we will send the current issue of our KTB Magazine to you by return email at no charge or obligation.

Or check our website............

www.sharkhunters.com

CPSIA information can be obtained at www.ICGtesting.com
Printed in the USA
LVOW01s2320090714

393594LV00028B/1067/P